"Tara Rethore and Catherine Langreney have nailed a huge challenge for new and aspiring CEOs. Bringing together strategy and operations is key to achieving the results you want in order to reach your destination. You'll want to refer to the tools repeatedly as new questions or challenges arise."

—Jeffrey Foster, Independent Board Member, Vault Digital Infrastructure and Broad Street Realty

"Many books and experts talk about CEO and C-suite leadership, but few give you the roadmap, lists, and tools to actually plan and execute. Tara and Catherine give you the tools to be flexible with today's rapid change and plan for the resilience to recover from setbacks. Add *Charting the Course* to your 'bag of tricks' whether you are a CEO or an advisor to the C-suite."

—Janeen Judah, Director, Patterson-UTI Energy, Crestwood Midstream, Aethon Energy, Jagged Peak Energy; former Executive, Chevron

"This book is the perfect resource for not only thinking about strategy, but also for doing it. The authors connect theory with what works on the ground to solve a variety of the most common business challenges. Few authors have tackled strategy development and execution in this way. This is a must read for CEOs and aspiring CEOs at startups to large corporations."

—Dr. Barbara Kurshan, Innovation Advisor, Penn GSE and Board Member, APEI

CHARTING THE COURSE:

CEO Tools to Align Strategy and Operations

Tara Rethore & Catherine Langreney

T&C Business Books and Media

Published by T & C Business Books and Media

ISBN #978-0-578-86304-7

Table of Contents

Foreword

When I met Catherine the first day of classes at our MBA program long ago, I had a strong feeling she would go on to accomplish great things. In the intervening 30 or so years, we have both served as CEOs in a wide variety of situations. While I was in Silicon Valley, Catherine and Tara worked at global companies to drive strategy and integrate execution. Catherine was in telecommunications and heavy industry; Tara in global energy and manufacturing; and me in technology and software. Our professional journeys have been very different, but we have all faced a strikingly similar set of challenges in the companies we've led or advised.

The words of Lewis Carroll, "If you don't know where you are going, any road will take you there," ring true to any CEO. Regardless of the company, the top issue I have repeatedly faced in taking on a new company is creating a clearly defined strategy, and a well-crafted operating plan to make it real. Both elements are critically important but taken independently they are each insufficient for success. The linkage of strategy and operations is where the real magic happens and defines your journey to success as a company.

Most business books deal with strategic or operational questions independently. Tara and Catherine take a different approach and pull these together. They provide a framework for thinking about and leading strategy, while also deliberately relating it to how the business must operate to successfully achieve the objectives. They connect theory with what works on the ground. While Tara and Catherine lay out a natural sequence for developing and executing strategy, they also recognize that strategy is an evolutionary process that develops while you are running your business. Their tools are accessible from multiple directions, depending on where you are in your strategic journey—and they're also relevant for such leaders as CEOs, GMs, Managing Directors, and country CEOs within larger organizations.

Charting the Course is a companion guide—a handy reference to use repeatedly to address new questions. It's also practical and can be applied to any business context. It brings together strategy and operations in a unique and compelling way, and it will be helpful for both sitting CEOs and those senior leaders who aspire to become CEOs.

Well done, Catherine and Tara!

Bill Gossman

Entrepreneur and CEO, HealthTap

Preface

Knowing where you want to go doesn't mean you always reach your destination.

We've all known what it is to encounter roadblocks and detours—even unexpected turbulence—on both personal and professional journeys. Being able to think on your feet and adapt to changing conditions separates those who successfully complete the journey from the ones who are derailed along the way.

For CEOs and senior executives, it's not enough to have a well thought-out strategy without a link to strong operational capabilities. Successful organizations rely on a solid combination of actionable strategy and operational depth.

That's why we wrote this book. Tara loves strategy; Catherine loves operations. Yet, we are each recognized for our experience in both areas. Most importantly, we realize that the magic really happens when both pieces—strategy and operations—come together effectively.

Our experiences are complementary. While we share common personal interests, we are also radically different. When we met, both of us were younger executives working in an old-school, international environment. Often, we were each tasked with driving major changes that weren't welcomed by much of the organization. That common ground between us made it easier to work collaboratively to find solutions. We tested ideas and quickly became brutally honest with each other about what worked—and what didn't.

We soon discovered that our different perspectives were a treasure trove, and tapping into that resource together was loads of fun. Meanwhile, we also juggled the needs of young families, working spouses with meaningful careers, and our own career aspirations. In many ways, we each became a lifeline for the other and, over time, we became companions along the journey.

Today, we derive great satisfaction from sharing what we've learned, creating what we wished we had available in our earlier careers, and helping other senior leaders to achieve their objectives with greater confidence. We also realize that not all senior leaders are equipped with strategic and operational skill sets in equal measure. Because we bring strategy and operations together, our compendium of resources expands your vision and experiences—no matter where you are in your own career or business journey.

Introduction

Translating strategic thinking into actions that work on the ground is one of the most challenging things senior leaders encounter in running their businesses.

In our experience, strategists are often encouraged to dream in order to drive forward thinking and aspiration. Operational[1] leaders are tasked with making it happen. Yet, too often, these activities are pursued independently. You've likely seen what happens when a strategic planning session is completed solely in the C-Suite, perhaps with the help of an external consultant and strategy expert. Afterwards, operational leaders receive the new strategy with a mandate to meet objectives. They must translate what the corporation has asked them to do into their own context and identify specific actions that make sense on the ground. In some ways, this demonstrates trust in operational leaders. In other ways, it sets them adrift—disconnecting CEOs and senior executives from the realities of effective operation and execution.

That's why we created this book—as a companion guide to help senior leaders like yourself take strategy forward more effectively. What if, instead of a rapid handoff from C-Suite to operations, CEOs took the time to explicitly connect strategy and operations? That would set the stage for the CEO to work with senior leaders to persistently and continuously maintain that connection.

Strategy, Mission, and Vision

Let's start with a shared definition of what we mean by strategy and operations, and their relationships to mission and vision. For us, **mission** is purpose. It's a simple, clear statement of *why* the organization exists. Mission rarely changes. For example, "The American Cancer Society's mission is to save lives, celebrate lives, and lead the fight for a world without cancer."[2]

Vision is the destination. It's *where* you want the organization to go or what it will achieve. A good vision contains an element of aspiration. By definition, a vision is future-oriented and will take at least a few years to achieve. For example, Walmart expresses its vision as: "Be *THE* destination for customers to save money, no matter how they want to shop." The Walmart vision complements their mission to "Save people money so they can live better."[3]

---

[1] Operational leaders include those who run business/product lines and functions (e.g., marketing, information technology, human resources, procurement, finance, legal, environmental health and safety, etc.).

[2] "Mission Statement," American Cancer Society, online. https://www.cancer.org/about-us/who-we-are/mission-statements.html

[3] Walmart Mission and Vision Statement Analysis, Walmart, online. https://mission-statement.com/walmart/

Strategy, then, is about *how*. It's the set of decisions and actions that get you where you want to go—or how you will achieve your vision. Typically, strategy describes the critical few priorities that guide the decisions. These should be forward-focused and, once set, not easily changed. Operations create the means through which you actually move; many tactics are operational in nature. Together, strategy and operations help you do what you set out to do. Planning is helpful for both, yet neither is simply about a plan. To reach your vision, both strategy and operations must be aligned and put into action.

> ## To reach your vision, both strategy and operations must be aligned and put into action.

In the first articulation of an enterprise strategy, CEOs explain the strategy and its connection to employees and customers. At the same time, it's important to be clear about how operations contribute to strategy—or the role operations plays in reaching the vision. Having been CEOs ourselves and worked with many more, we know that this step is critical. Many CEOs and senior leaders recognize it as such. Still, the importance of doing this well can't be overstated. Rather than delivering a slide deck describing objectives, it's important to engage senior leaders in an active conversation to answer questions and constantly seek clarity. Then, all senior leaders can define their own departmental visions within the context of the larger enterprise vision and describe their contributions to the overall strategy. That creates the link between strategy and operations.

The Obvious Can Be Difficult

The need to align strategy and operations may seem obvious. Yet, in practice it's often more difficult to do, as we have learned personally.

Catherine arrived as a new CEO in a developing country—charged with defining and executing a growth strategy to take advantage of the rapidly growing economy and to drive demand for the company's product.

The business was already well-established, yet its potential had not been fully tapped. It benefited from a highly concentrated, oligopolistic structure and an underserved market. Very little product differentiation among the current players offered opportunity which, when combined with the growing economy, attracted new entrants.

While on the surface, growth might have seemed easy, other factors assured it was not. A scarce talent pool plus production facilities in need of upgrade made it more challenging to compete against new, state-of-the-art facilities introduced by the new players. Catherine needed not only to develop a compelling new vision (to set the destination), she also had to put everything in place to make it happen. That meant undoing old ways of working and producing, rather than starting from scratch.

Like other CEOs in Catherine's shoes, she quickly realized that strategy and operations must be synchronized. The dynamic market meant that external forces were constantly in flux. Success required regular checks of both strategy and operations to assure alignment and make adjustments. It was simply not possible to drive strategy forward (a typical role for the CEO) without in-depth, deliberate, and regular understanding of what was happening on the ground.

Meanwhile, in her consulting work, Tara has advised senior leaders as they discovered the lack of balance between strategy and operations in their businesses.

For example, the new CEO of an established US-based product and service company was hired to accelerate growth and dramatically increase revenue while maintaining profitability. Acquisition was an option, but only if the acquired company could show immediate and ongoing results. Investors also did not have the patience to wait for acquisitions to demonstrate growth. As a result, acquisition was unlikely to be the sole growth strategy. Additional drags included a long lead-time to create new products with a highly concentrated customer base, and few barriers to entry that encouraged new competitors in multiple parts of their value chain.

The CEO quickly realized that he needed not only a new strategy, but also a different approach to defining the strategy and involving the leadership team in the process. Like Catherine, he soon realized he also needed to align strategy and operations in order to demonstrate the value of the new destination and create an attractive path forward for investors. The "aha" moment for the team was realizing that what they were doing on the ground was inconsistent with what they wanted or needed to do to reach the destination. The CEO needed external help in clarifying the destination, identifying the key strategic priorities to close the gaps between where they were and where they wanted to be, and setting in motion the disciplines and tools to actively manage the balance between strategy and operations.

In these two examples, both CEOs realized they could benefit from practical tools and external support to help them align strategy and operations. We share these particular examples because they are typical of the situations we've encountered throughout our careers. Both of us have worked in a broad range of industries and organizations of varying sizes around the globe. We've held roles ranging from functional to purely operational, strategic, or entrepreneurial. Over the years, though our individual journeys diverged, we realized how deeply aligned we are, particularly about the incredible power of the marriage of strategy and operations. This knowledge and expertise are both critical for CEOs to be successful.

Mapping the Journey

Charting the Course is a set of tools that make you think, help you plan, and spur action. None of our tools is industry specific. They work—or can be adapted—for any context to facilitate your journey or address a specific challenge you may face. This is a companion guide for leaders, written in a conversational way. It's that voice on your shoulder or that resource you tap when you don't know what you don't know—or when you need a little extra support to put together the whys, whats, and hows of running your business. That's what it means to balance and align strategic thinking with operational realities.

> *Charting the Course* **is a set of tools that make you think, help you plan, and spur action.**

While we often refer to the CEO for simplicity, the tools in this book are valuable not only for Chief Executives, but for other senior management leaders as well.

Introducing the Tools

Section 1: Set the Destination

External Landscape
Bringing together what you know about your business context

Effective Decisions
Introducing decision frameworks

Visioning
Setting the destination—where do you want to go

Onboarding
Onboarding leadership team members

Current Reality
Establishing shared understanding of where you are right now

Section 2: Plan the Journey

Competitive Positioning
Understanding where you fit versus competition

Strategic Planning
Setting high-level strategic priorities to close gaps and detailing specific action plans

Risk Assessment
Identifying exposure to potential risks and establishing practices to mitigate them

Value Propositions
Describing the value of your products and services for target customer groups

Strategic Dashboard
Setting interim strategic targets and illuminating progress toward them

Gap Analysis
Understanding the critical gaps in your capabilities versus what's required for success

Capital Investment Visibility
Creating value through planning and monitoring CapEx

Section 3: Manage Your Journey

Operational Execution
Executing specific operational targets and actions that underpin the strategic priorities

Organizational Capabilities Assessment
Assessing ongoing readiness of the organization to reach the destination

Performance Management
Assessing individual capabilities to achieve objectives at regular intervals

Crisis Management
Creating the building blocks to navigate crisis situations

Strong Board Relations
Leveraging the expertise and contribution of your board of directors or advisors

Section 4: Sustain the Pace

Elements of Culture
Assessing, creating, and nurturing the culture you need

High Performance Teams
Developing and leading exceptional teams

Strategic Communication
Designing and delivering messages that connect people to your vision and strategy

Feedback
Giving and receiving feedback well to support and sustain progress toward your vision

Rhythm & Pace
Managing your organization's momentum in reaching the destination

Section 5: Reach Your Destination

Vision Accomplished
Knowing when to declare victory— or reset the destination

What We Have Learned
Taking time to reflect and learn before launching the next new initiative

Retooling
Identifying and investing in the tools, approaches, and capabilities needed to pursue the next destination

About The Book

As a companion guide, *Charting the Course* is designed to help senior leaders who are certain about many things, uncertain about some, and eager to learn about still more. Building on and sharing our own experience, we help you to ask new questions, discover things you hadn't considered in your current context, or bring different tools and approaches to the forefront. Our tools guide you along the journey you're setting for your business. That journey is essentially the path you will take to reach the objectives you've set for the business. Whether it's visioning to set your destination, assessing risks, onboarding new team members, managing crises, determining when you've reached the destination, or anything in between—we've got you covered. By bringing together strategy and operations in one resource, we make it easier to keep both in gear—interlocked and moving in the same direction.

Running a business today is vastly different from doing so a decade ago—or perhaps even as little as six months ago. It seems to be a universal truth that the world keeps moving faster and business must keep up or fall by the wayside. Yet, in our experience, it's not just about velocity; complexity is also a major challenge. Even in small businesses, the complexity of work is greater than ever before.[4] Scanning the news, it's hard not to find an article about the latest disruption. Disruptions appear to be more prevalent and significant. In our work with other senior leaders, many of us find it increasingly difficult to know which disruptions are the most real or lasting. At the time of this writing, the world is embroiled in a global health crisis[5] that has fundamentally shifted ways of working, living, and interacting with others. The near-term impacts are far-reaching and significant.

The longer-term path as yet remains unclear. How do we know when to shift direction or continue on our current path?

Not long ago, our work and work-related decisions were organized around hierarchical structures. Today, cross-functional teams are much more common, with an emphasis on collaboration and active, dynamic problem solving. For the last several years, collaboration has been largely in-person, or via co-located teams. The world has now moved more substantively and comprehensively to telework, remote teaming, and the use of online tools. Collaboration and interpersonal connections become both more important and more challenging to manage.

---

[4] For example, see these articles discussing the growing complexity and its impact for leaders: Lucas Smith, "How are You Managing Increasing Complexity in Your Work?" *Skyline Technologies Blog,* 2017. https://www.skylinetechnologies.com/Blog/Skyline-Blog/November_2017/how-are-you-managing-complexity-work; and Lynda Gratton, "Leading in Complex Times" Harvard Business Review, 2013. https://hbr.org/2013/10/leading-in-complex-times.

[5] The COVID-19 virus began spreading through Asia in 2019, and reached global pandemic proportions in 2020.

[6] AGILE is not an acronym, although it's generally written in all caps. The term originated as a set of principles for software development but is now applied to many other aspects of managing business operations and projects. AGILE concepts promote adaptive planning, early delivery, continuous improvement, and rapid and flexible response to change. AGILE is highly dependent on teams, and it promotes self-organization and cross-functional participation.

Work today also requires agility, which is simply the ability to shift direction quickly and smoothly. That has spawned both behavioral changes in our leadership style and more formal approaches, such as AGILE[6] project management. Our workforce includes multiple generations, with varied expectations and ways of working—the implications of which we've yet to fully comprehend. In many countries (though perhaps most keenly in the US), we've come to realize that diversity matters and true inclusion is far more difficult to achieve than it should be. Businesses and economies benefit when individuals are treated equitably and are afforded the same opportunities and respect. How do we structure our businesses and organizations to respect differences, incorporate varied ideas and concepts, and foster cross-generational collaboration?

Today, we have more tools and technology available that make it easier to connect with customers and colleagues, to share information, and to collect and understand data. Yet, having so many options can make it difficult to determine which tool is best for each purpose and then to make the best use of the tools and resources we already have. How do we choose?

These types of decisions are just some of the twists CEOs and senior leaders must navigate on the road to successful destinations. In addition, each industry and organization type also encounters its own kinds of roadblocks and opportunities. By the time you are reading this overview, new factors will have emerged.

That's why each section suggests critical questions and provides tools to help you address them. We look across the key facets of business – strategy, operations, capital (money), and people – and deal with the interdependencies. *Charting the Course* addresses five areas that have a significant impact on your ability to continue delivering on what's happening now, while also driving toward the future you've defined. Take a look:

Journey Map

Section 1:
Set the
Destination

- Understand your external landscape—industry trends, drivers of change, opportunities, and threats—and current reality
- Set your vision (destination)
- Get everyone on the same page

Section 2:
Plan the
Journey

- Assess competitive position and internal capabilities (strengths and weaknesses)
- Describe your value proposition
- Identify critical gaps between where you are and your vision
- Define strategic priorities and the plan to close gaps and monitor progress

Section 3:
Manage the
Journey

- Link specific actions to high level strategic priorities
- Assess the ongoing performance of the organization and individuals
- Leverage your Board
- Navigate crises effectively

Section 4:
Sustain the
Pace

- Create an environment that fosters high performance and attention to people
- Attend to cultural elements and strategic communication
- Set and manage the rhythm and pace of the organization

Section 5:
Reach Your Destination

- Know when you've achieved the vision, what you've learned, and how to retool the organization before starting a new strategic initiative

While these are the key components required for any journey, they are not always used sequentially. Much depends on where you are at any given point in the journey. A number of components may be iterative. The learning you develop as you travel or continue on your way—plus changes in landscape, competitive positions, or market and customer needs—require rethinking your approach. With those lessons, you adjust the tactics, decisions, and actions needed to achieve your vision.

We've applied that same idea to the structure of this book. We liken the five areas to the steps you take on a journey to reach a compelling vision—that's your destination. We've also identified a number of challenges that CEOs and their teams commonly face at various points along the way. You may choose to access the tools from either perspective, or to dive more deeply into a specific area as needed.

The first step in any journey is knowing where you are today. There are two common starting points:

I know where I am in the journey to reach the destination.

Great! The flow of the book suggests a sequence. In practice, however, the tools can be used in any order—because not every business starts from the same place or has all the same pieces fully in place, all the time. Start with the section and tools that reflect your current position and move on from there. You may also find moving forward requires revisiting earlier parts of your journey to ensure that your team shares your understanding of where you are. Either way, *Charting the Course* works.

I want to address a specific challenge that I'm facing now or anticipating I will face soon.

We've captured common challenges CEOs face and mapped the tools that may help to address them. Find the challenge that's closest to the one you face and review the suggested tools. You may find your challenge is a hybrid or combination of several common challenges. In that case, dive more deeply into the relevant tools or sections to identify new techniques or how you might improve on what you're currently doing.

Common CEO Challenges

Your growth has hit a plateau. You want to take it to the next level.

You're not sure if your team has a clear and shared understanding of what it will take to achieve the objectives.

Your team seems to be constantly playing catch-up; you're regularly fighting fires and reacting, rather than anticipating trends, changes, opportunities, challenges.

Your team is mired in the daily demands of the business, leaving little space to pursue the long-term objectives.

You're surrounded by stakeholders with competing agendas that get in the way or slow progress toward the vision.

You're not sure if your company environment is conducive to achieving your ambition.

You're not sure that you have the right capabilities and processes to scale up the business and fuel the next stage of growth.

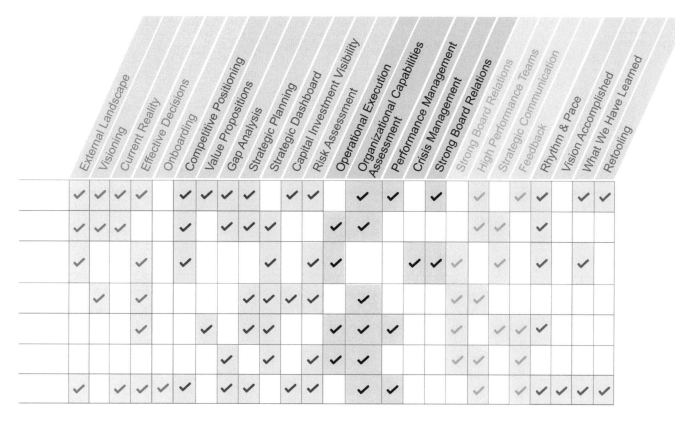

Section 1:
Set the Destination

Section 2:
Plan the Journey

Section 3:
Manage the Journey

Section 4:
Sustain the Pace

Section 5:
Reach the Destination

You feel you've gone as far as the organization can go to meet the current ambition, and now need to prepare the team for the next phase.

You're dependent on a few critical customers or a particular agreement; or you want to diversify your customer mix.

You feel like you are swimming upstream without a team to support and advise you.

Your board members or your team do not understand your business strategy or opportunity for value creation.

You are not sure the right information is flowing upward allowing you to engage stakeholders and to make good decisions.

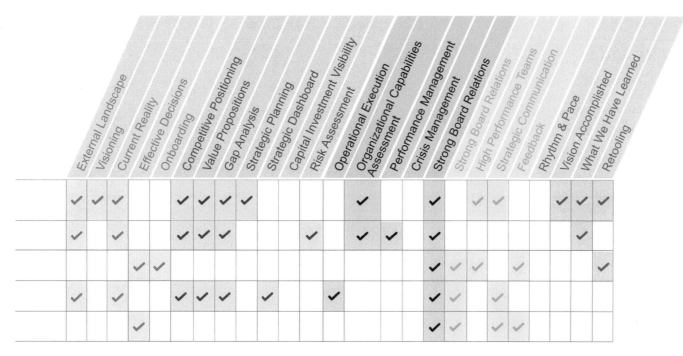

Section 1:
Set the Destination

Section 2:
Plan the Journey

Section 3:
Manage the Journey

Section 4:
Sustain the Pace

Section 5:
Reach the Destination

Agility and Flexibility

In our experience, finding the right balance of strategy and operations requires agility. The book is designed to facilitate fluid movement among all tools and to accommodate a variety of business journeys, regardless of your current position or challenge.

Charting the Course contains 25 tools, and is organized to help address strategic and operational questions or challenges. Managing your business is rarely split so nicely between the two; that's why alignment and balance become so critical. Overall, you need both; yet at any given moment, a focus on either strategy or operations may be more necessary. Similarly, each tool sits on the spectrum between strategy and operations, and at times, they toggle between the two. That structure gives you the flexibility you need to adapt the tools to best suit your specific situation.

We guide you through each Section—each step in your strategic journey—with an overview and tips to dive into the relevant tools. We then define each tool in the Section and suggest how you can apply the tool effectively. We include a **Roadmap** (an outline of the steps you take to implement the tool), additional context, and **Aids** and **Examples** that support you as you move through the **Roadmap**. These are practical frameworks that translate theory into action, so that you can tailor the tools to your situation. At the end of each tool, you'll find **Acceleration Tips** to improve your performance or use of the tool. Throughout the book, we use common icons to identify each element and to help you to navigate the tools.

Ready? Fasten your seatbelt and let's get started.

Section 1: Set the Destination

Travel for the sheer joy of traveling can be exciting and wonderfully appealing: you are creating the rules and forging ahead into the relative unknown.

Many CEOs and entrepreneurs do just that, fueled by a fundamental belief in their business concept and their ability to "figure it all out" as they go. Often, that approach works for a while, but becomes increasingly difficult to manage as the business grows and the environment becomes more volatile.

> **While you need a clear destination, it's also important to understand the broader context.**

This is when you need a clear destination: where are you going? It's also important to understand the broader context. On a journey, you need at least a sense of the environment or landscape—including the potential hazards you may encounter or what it's like to travel in that area. If you are traveling with others, you also need a shared understanding of both the destination and the starting point.

In business, we've found it's helpful to start with a conversation that's focused on specific, well-articulated outcomes, and to ask a few key questions. Our Tools will help you to address those questions as you set your destination. Perhaps start with these:

Questions to consider:

- **In what ways might the dynamics of our world, customers, or industry change? What's driving those changes?**
- **What opportunities and threats for our business arise from this understanding of our world?**
- **Where do we see our company in 5 years?**
- **What does success look like in 3 years? In 5 years?**
- **Do we have a good understanding of our current reality?**
- **How do we ensure that our senior leaders hit the ground running?**
- **How will we take decisions?**

How To Use The Tools To Set The Destination:

This section contains Tools to help you balance strategy and operations from the very beginning. From a strategic standpoint, first articulate your vision—that's where you want to go. The **Visioning Tool** helps you do this, and ensures everyone has the same understanding of what that destination actually looks like. Your vision benefits from a clear assessment of the context in which your business operates. That's the **External Landscape**, including the opportunities and threats for your industry.

You and your team may already have a sense of where you are right now. If so, great! It's helpful to describe that in a consistent way. That is your **Current Reality**. Remember: your strategy is the set of decisions and actions that close the gap between where you are (the current reality) and where you're going (destination/vision). Use the **Current Reality Tool** to develop a consistent understanding of your current strengths and weaknesses, focusing on those that are most relevant to the opportunities and threats identified in the **External Landscape Tool**. That makes it easier to take[1] decisions about what the team will do to close the gaps. Those strategic priorities also guide operational choices (e.g., retooling, enhanced operating capacity, new capabilities, different teaming or organizational structures, etc.)

In our experience, we find it's often unclear *how* the organization takes decisions. Thus, we have included the **Effective Decisions Tool** to frame and take decisions consistently and effectively. As the senior leader, you offer a framework for decisions and encourage your team to shape their questions or challenges in terms of the decisions you (or others) must take. By adopting a consistent framework, you also give others a better sense of their role in the decision.

It's critical to onboard people effectively—to get them up to speed on where you are going, the ways in which you work, and where you are in the journey. That's why we've included the **Onboarding Tool**. This will make it easier for them to contribute both strategically and operationally. They'll know what's expected and the role they will play in executing the strategy.

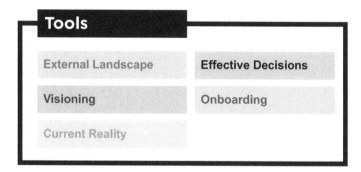

Tools

External Landscape	Effective Decisions
Visioning	Onboarding
Current Reality	

---

[1]Throughout the book, we refer to taking decisions rather than making them. It's more than semantics. Certainly, leaders at any level regularly make decisions. Unfortunately, not everyone owns the decisions they make. We've learned that when a leader takes a decision—and uses that terminology—it suggests ownership of the decision and a commitment to its impact or consequence. Some decisions are simply made. Others require more deliberate ownership and emphasis; those are the decisions leaders take.

Dive into the Tools:

External Landscape

Often referred to as the macro-environment, the external landscape includes all the conditions outside your company's direct control, yet which have a meaningful impact on the business. This includes such factors as the legal framework, political or regulatory climate, local or national economy, social trends and forces, environmental mandates or preferences, technological events, access to funding—and more. The external landscape reflects the larger context in which your company operates and your customers buy.

Thus, we recommend starting with a thorough review and understanding of your external landscape—as an input to visioning and before developing strategy. It's a necessary and critical step in crafting strategies to capture opportunities, overcome competition, and reduce the effects of external threats.

> Looking externally first expands your thinking and creates space and skill to avoid myopia. It also improves the quality of your assessment of internal capabilities—your strengths and weaknesses.

Note two important words we've used: opportunities and threats. These are the "O" and "T" indicated in a traditional SWOT[2] analysis—a very common strategy tool. And while the acronym, SWOT, rolls off the tongue easily, we'd argue there's value in shifting the order—from SWOT to OTSW. Why? The "O" and "T" in that analysis are externally facing. They add a future and outward aspect to your thinking, which is particularly helpful in visioning. That external focus ensures you are scanning the environment broadly, looking for what's possible and what could change—rather than dwelling on what's real, right now.

In contrast, the "S" and "W" are internally facing, as they relate to the strengths and weaknesses of your company. These are best considered later, and in the context of the opportunities and threats you've identified. Both perspectives are important, of course. In our experience, looking externally first expands your thinking and creates space and skill to avoid myopia. It also improves the quality of your assessment of internal capabilities—your strengths and weaknesses. (See the **Current Reality Tool** for more on those.)

---

[2]Per Wikipedia, a SWOT analysis is "an initialism for strengths, weaknesses, opportunities, and threats." https://en.wikipedia.org/wiki/SWOT-analysis

ROADMAP

Three steps to gain a collective understanding of the external context

External Landscape

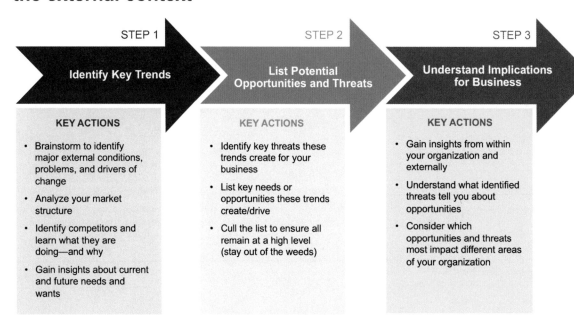

STEP 1

Identify Key Trends

KEY ACTIONS

- Brainstorm to identify major external conditions, problems, and drivers of change

- Analyze your market structure

- Identify competitors and learn what they are doing—and why

- Gain insights about current and future needs and wants

STEP 2

List Potential Opportunities and Threats

KEY ACTIONS

- Identify key threats these trends create for your business

- List key needs or opportunities these trends create/drive

- Cull the list to ensure all remain at a high level (stay out of the weeds)

STEP 3

Understand Implications for Business

KEY ACTIONS

- Gain insights from within your organization and externally

- Understand what identified threats tell you about opportunities

- Consider which opportunities and threats most impact different areas of your organization

Note: Strengths and weaknesses are internally facing. Thus, they are not needed when considering the external landscape.

Brainstorming trends, then sorting and grouping results, is often the best way to make sense of your external landscape. Consider whether the potential opportunities and threats you've identified are seen from the right vantage point—at 30,000-foot Enterprise level, not the tactical ground level. The goal is to expand your thinking. We want you to understand the bigger picture. Diving too deeply into the details inhibits that. As the **External Landscape Roadmap** suggests, it's all about understanding what these insights tell you about your business. How might these impact your choice of destination (vision) and the subsequent decisions and actions you will take (strategy)?

While we list **External Landscape** first—because it immediately shifts attention to the future and things outside of your organization—it's actually a powerful tool to use throughout your strategy journey. We reference this tool multiple times throughout the book. Ideally, you will monitor the external landscape regularly to capitalize on opportunities, avoid or mitigate threats, and adapt your decisions and actions accordingly. We've included two **Aids** to help you structure your data for ease of analysis. Check the **Acceleration Tips** before you begin.

AID

The STEEP framework can provide a structured way to:

1. Organize and characterize your external landscape
2. Identify drivers of change

Social – Buying trends, lifestyle, media, major events, etc.

Technological – Innovations, access to technology, licensing & patents, R&D funding, manufacturing, etc.

Economic – Taxes, interest rates, inflation, consumer confidence, financial markets

Environmental – Local, regional or global issues, including, but not limited to, sustainability and green factors

Political – Legal, regulatory, policy trends, or issues that may impact your business

Note: Choose the analogous PEST tool when there is no need to distinguish among environmental factors which may impact your business or industry

External Landscape

 AID

Consider what emerging trends suggest about potential *opportunities and threats*.

1. Brainstorm Potential Opportunities

DO	ASK	RESULT: OPPORTUNITIES LIST
• Identify key drivers of change in your macro environment • Consider what opportunities these key change drivers could suggest • Identify key enablers	• What can you learn from recent entrants into your market? • What role exists for standard vs. custom solutions? • How do you leverage your know-how? • What helps you access these opportunities?	For example: ✓ Low barriers to entry in your prospective market ✓ Rapid adoption rate among customers ✓ Very strong GDP and infrastructure investment ✓ Easy access to qualified talent

Tip: Make sure these are all company level (30,000-foot) opportunities or threats

2. Brainstorm Potential Threats

DO	ASK	RESULT: THREATS LIST
• Return to key drivers of change • Remember: A threat is not merely the inverse of opportunity • Look for threats from unexpected places	• What threats do these pose for you now? • What threats might emerge? • What can disrupt your world? • What should be on your watch list? • What gives you pause?	For example: ✓ Many small newcomers ✓ Production tool obsolescence ✓ New customer acquisition cost rising fast ✓ Major tax overhaul

External Landscape

ACCELERATION TIPS

When brainstorming, remember it's about the conversation and understanding—not about making a list.

- Keep it simple and at a relatively high level
- Anticipate the speed bumps

Get the big picture via PEST or STEEP analysis – *before* developing OT.

- Ensure you have identified the right external drivers of opportunities or threats
- Obtain additional perspectives from external thinkers

When considering implications of these external factors on your business or industry, rank them by greatest or least certainty.

- Focus on the possibilities and opportunities these changes might create

Good sources of data: Industry/financial analysts, newspapers, publications, trade organizations, government agencies, etc.

Visioning

Regardless of where you are now, you can't get 'there' if you don't know where the destination is. In that case, there's no 'there,' there.

As we've already noted, vision is essential for strategy as it defines where you want to go, or what you intend to achieve or do. It's your destination. Visioning allows you and your team to consider the *possibilities* for your business, rather than getting stuck in what your business and industry look like today or what's just over the horizon.

> **Vision is essential for strategy as it defines where you want to go, or what you intend to achieve or do. It's your destination.**

Using the insights gained from considering your **External Landscape**, dream with your leadership team about what 'could be' for your organization. Better yet, include critical stakeholders or thought leaders in your visioning sessions to enhance the quality of the vision and assure a *shared understanding* of that vision. Set a specific timeframe within which to achieve the vision. There is no magic timeframe, but it should be at least a few years out. Select a year that's close enough to the present to feel relevant and generate a sense of urgency, yet far enough into the future to allow stretch.

Our **Visioning Roadmap** describes the three steps needed to create a shared vision. Importantly, the value is in the *conversation*. You are thinking and crafting the vision together, melding ideas, and drafting a statement that captures what the group means when it talks about vision.

 ROADMAP

Start with mission. Focus on 'what could be,' not 'what is.'

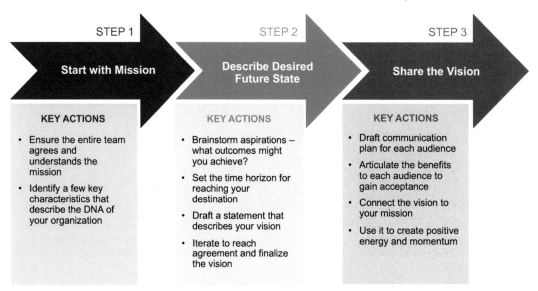

STEP 1

Start with Mission

KEY ACTIONS

- Ensure the entire team agrees and understands the mission
- Identify a few key characteristics that describe the DNA of your organization

STEP 2

Describe Desired Future State

KEY ACTIONS

- Brainstorm aspirations – what outcomes might you achieve?
- Set the time horizon for reaching your destination
- Draft a statement that describes your vision
- Iterate to reach agreement and finalize the vision

STEP 3

Share the Vision

KEY ACTIONS

- Draft communication plan for each audience
- Articulate the benefits to each audience to gain acceptance
- Connect the vision to your mission
- Use it to create positive energy and momentum

Remember, vision is not mission. Mission is about purpose. Distinguishing between the two is often tricky in organizations. And both are founded upon the organization's *values*—which describe your collective beliefs and are demonstrated by how all employees behave. The following table offers a snapshot of these key terms.

 TABLE

Clarify Your Terms

	Mission	Vision	Values	Strategy
	Purpose	*Destination*	*Beliefs*	*Decisions & Actions*
Answers the questions	Why do we exist? What is our purpose? What do we want to be known for?	Where do we want to go? What do we aspire to be or do?	What do we believe? What guides our behaviors?	How will we get to where we want to go?
Spans this timeframe	A mission statement is anchored in the present leading to the future	A vision statement projects your future	Values are timeless	It reflects the time needed to move from the present to your aspired future
Passes the litmus test	What do we do today? For whom? What is the benefit? Why we do what we do? For whom do we do this and to what end?	Where do we see ourselves in 5+ years? What do we hope for? What does success look like?	What traits embody what's best about our organization? Has this been present in our organization for a long time (core) or is this something we need to work hard to cultivate (aspirational)?	What decisions and actions will close the gaps between where we are and where we hope to be?

The **Visioning Session Aids** walk through possible conversations you might lead to establish your shared vision, including examples of strong visions and missions.

In the end, keep it simple. Your vision should roll off the tongue with ease, so that everyone in the organization can remember it, talk about it, and embrace it meaningfully as they take decisions, interact with customers, and do their jobs.

AID

Establishing a shared vision: The value is in the conversation.

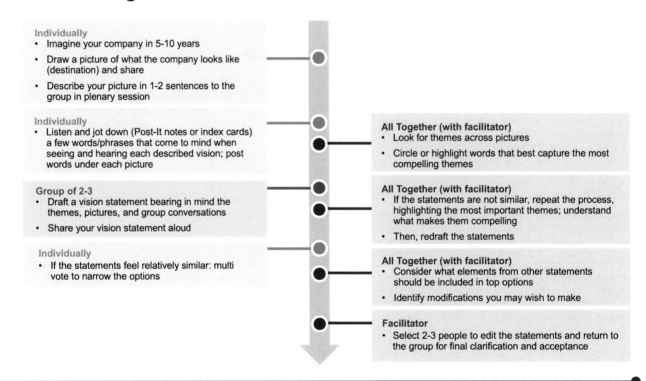

Visioning

Individually
- Imagine your company in 5-10 years
- Draw a picture of what the company looks like (destination) and share
- Describe your picture in 1-2 sentences to the group in plenary session

Individually
- Listen and jot down (Post-It notes or index cards) a few words/phrases that come to mind when seeing and hearing each described vision; post words under each picture

All Together (with facilitator)
- Look for themes across pictures
- Circle or highlight words that best capture the most compelling themes

Group of 2-3
- Draft a vision statement bearing in mind the themes, pictures, and group conversations
- Share your vision statement aloud

All Together (with facilitator)
- If the statements are not similar, repeat the process, highlighting the most important themes; understand what makes them compelling
- Then, redraft the statements

Individually
- If the statements feel relatively similar: multi vote to narrow the options

All Together (with facilitator)
- Consider what elements from other statements should be included in top options
- Identify modifications you may wish to make

Facilitator
- Select 2-3 people to edit the statements and return to the group for final clarification and acceptance

AID

Use a vision board to establish a shared vision.

Vision Board			
Team Member 1	*Team Member 2*	*Team Member 3*	*Team Member 4*

Imagine your company in 5-10 years

Draw a picture of what the company will look like and share/post for all to see

Describe your picture in 1-2 sentences (each person shares verbally with the whole group)

By 2025 we will be launching a satellite

Listen to the descriptions. Jot down on Post-It notes words or phrases that come to mind when seeing and hearing each of the described visions

Post your words under each picture

First global coverage

Together: Look for themes across all the pictures. Consider which are most compelling and why.

Visioning

Examples of Mission Statements

PBS	We create content that educates, informs, and inspires
Google	We organize the world's information and make it universally accessible and useful
Make-A-Wish	Together, we create life-changing wishes for children with critical illnesses
Southwest Airline	Dedication to the highest quality of service delivered with a sense of warmth, friendliness, individual pride, and COMPANY SPIRIT and CUSTOMER SERVICE
General Motors	To earn customers for life by building brands and inspire passion and loyalty through not only breakthrough technologies, but also by serving and improving the communities in which we live and work around the world
Samsung	We will devote our human resources and technology to create superior products and services, thereby contributing to a better global society

Visioning

Examples of Vision Statements

Ford	To become the world's leading consumer company for automotive products and services
Google	To provide access to the world in one click
Make-A-Wish	We are dedicated to making every eligible child's wish come true
Southwest Airline	To become the world's most loved, most flown, most profitable airline
General Motors	To become the world's most valued automotive company
Samsung	To inspire the world with our innovative technologies, products, and designs that enrich people's lives and contribute to social prosperity by creating a new future

Visioning

ACCELERATION TIPS

Know your mission before drafting your vision.

- If your team doesn't already understand and articulate mission in the same way, start over.

Make sure your passions are reflected in the vision.

Try working backwards: Imagine a world where you've achieved your organization's vision.

- Of what are you most proud?
- Whom are you serving? What are you doing (or not doing)?
- What benefit or value do you offer?
- What was the most significant breakthrough that got you here?
- What will be the same as today? What will be different?

Consider having pictures on hand to spark vision ideas, rather than requiring people to draw their vision.

Remember: The best visions are not boring.

- They're difficult to achieve, meaningful to the whole organization, and motivational
- They don't require eloquence: be simple, direct, and explicit

Current Reality

It's always a good idea to ensure the team has a shared understanding of the business as it is today. That's your current reality—your starting line.

 ROADMAP

Take a broad view of the organization to create a comprehensive picture of your starting line.

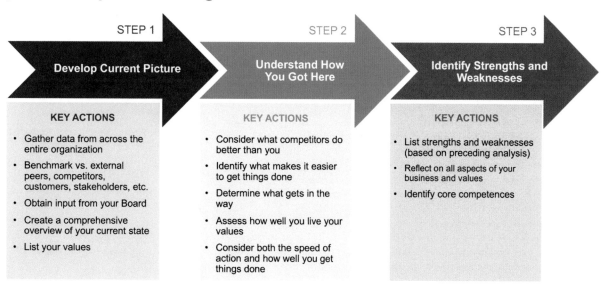

STEP 1	STEP 2	STEP 3
Develop Current Picture	**Understand How You Got Here**	**Identify Strengths and Weaknesses**
KEY ACTIONS	**KEY ACTIONS**	**KEY ACTIONS**
• Gather data from across the entire organization • Benchmark vs. external peers, competitors, customers, stakeholders, etc. • Obtain input from your Board • Create a comprehensive overview of your current state • List your values	• Consider what competitors do better than you • Identify what makes it easier to get things done • Determine what gets in the way • Assess how well you live your values • Consider both the speed of action and how well you get things done	• List strengths and weaknesses (based on preceding analysis) • Reflect on all aspects of your business and values • Identify core competences

The **Current Reality Roadmap** is fairly straightforward to follow. Yet, once again, the power is in the conversation and taking a more holistic view of your business. We also provide a common framework to form a more complete picture of your financial situation, operating status, and overall capabilities. Unlike the **External Landscape Tool**, the **Current Reality Tool** looks predominantly at your *internal capabilities*—your strengths and weaknesses, or the 'S' and 'W' in a SWOT or OTSW analysis. While it's just a snapshot, it's also the starting point for identifying the gaps that may inhibit your ability to achieve the vision.

Fortunately, numerous frameworks already exist to help you assess your current reality. There's no need to reinvent the wheel! Use the approach that suits your purpose and feels right for your organization. We've assembled a **Key Resources Aid** showing the key purpose or application of some of the more common resources you may already use, know, or can readily find.

Importantly, **Current Reality** includes more than numbers. It's equally important to understand how you work (processes, inventory management, information sharing, etc.) and make decisions. Much has been written about the importance of understanding how the organization really operates—perhaps most fittingly captured as *The Unwritten Rules of the Game*,[3] by Peter Scott-Morgan. In his seminal book, Scott-Morgan asserts that the silent engine in any organization is not the official policies, but the unwritten rules. Deciphering those rules—or understanding how things really work—reveals why people work and behave the way they do. It can also tell you the extent to which your organization truly lives its values. In turn, that generates insights about deeply rooted strengths or weaknesses that can meaningfully impact your success in achieving the vision.

Once you've gathered the data, be sure to assess both efficiency—how *easily* you get things done—and effectiveness—how *well* you get them done. You are probably already using several metrics to measure both efficiency and effectiveness for financial and operating practices. Use the **Organizational Effectiveness Assessment Aid** to understand organizational effectiveness and discern what it might mean for your readiness to achieve the vision.

Next, test your own assumptions or interpretations by including customer or supplier input, and benchmarking against competitors. That puts your performance and capabilities into a broader, outward-facing context—and helps you avoid navel-gazing. Once complete, you'll understand your current reality and, thus, your starting line. It tells you where you are, right now. Later, you'll use the results from this assessment of your current reality to help identify critical gaps in capabilities.

---

[3] Peter Scott-Morgan, *The Unwritten Rules of the Game* (McGraw-Hill), 1994.

AID

Current Reality — Key Resources

Don't reinvent the wheel. Use the tool that suits your purpose and feels right for your organization.

Purpose or Step	Tools & Resources
Assessing overall business	STaRS Model - Michael Watkins' *The First 90 Days*, Table 3-1 and Figure 3-1
Competitive environment	Michael Porter's *Five Forces*
Assessing customer satisfaction, needs, or wants	Customer satisfaction surveys, independent polls, market research, etc.
Financial strength	Financials and internal audit reports Analyst reports (esp. for public companies)
Operational efficiency & effectiveness	Internal KPIs, operating reports, scorecards, etc.
Assessing organizational efficiency	Human resources statistics for operational HR activities End-to-end process analysis/KPIs (e.g., Service Level Agreement data)
Assessing organizational morale	Employee satisfaction or engagement surveys, internal polls, online blogs, etc.

Sources: Michael Watkins, *The First 90 Days: Proven Strategies for Getting Up to Speed Faster and Smarter* (Harvard Business School Press), 2013, Table 3-1 and Figure 3-1.

Michael Porter, *Five Forces: Understand competitive forces and stay ahead of the competition* (50Minutes.com), 2015.

Current Reality

 AID

Organizational Effectiveness Assessment

Section/Number	Question	Answers	
		Agree	Disagree
Section A	**Defining Organizational Effectiveness**		
1	I am clear on the mission for my organization		
2	I can translate that mission into the goals and results required		
3	I can translate those results into what I need to do in my specific role		
4	I can translate the mission into leadership and team behaviours required of me		
Section B	**Measuring Organizational Effectiveness**		
1	I am clear on the performance objectives and standards for my function		
2	I am clear on my decision making authorities		
3	I understand 'what good looks like' for my function		
4	I am clear on my roles and responsibilities and accountabilities		
5	I am clear on who I need to collaborate with to be successful in my role		
6	My teams feel 'empowered' and supported to make decisions		
7	We follow through on promises and commitments to next steps		

Current Reality

Section/ Number	Question	Answers	
		Agree	Disagree
Section C	**Managing the 'White Spaces'**		
1	The operating culture supports solving root causes, not just symptoms		
2	I would describe my function as 'implementation oriented'		
3	Priorities for immediate action are clear		
4	We build time and forum for assessing and embedding learning		
5	There are mechanisms in place to formally support collaboration		
6	I have developed a personal network with whom I collaborate		
7	I can channel my ideas and creative thoughts to those who make the policies and decisions		
8	You can feel the 'hum' in my function		
Section D	**Describing My Effectiveness**		
1	I would describe myself as an 'implementer'		
2	I would describe myself as 'planner'		
3	I am consulted on matters outside of my formal role/job		
4	I have a high level of confidence in my ability to make the right decisions		
5	I know where to find the information I need		
6	I am working a level above my current roles and authorities		
7	Others recognize the passion that I have for what I do		

Current Reality

Source: Tara J Rethore, Strategy for Real and Marian Bradshaw-Knapton, Avocet Organizational Performance. 2008. Used with permission.

AID

Organizational Effectiveness Assessment

What it all means…

The road to organizational effectiveness is not a casual journey along a one-way, well-marked autobahn. Rather, it's fraught with bumps, twists, turns, and often, a few 'wrong ways.' Once you've set the direction (strategy), you must ensure the mechanics are in place and well-oiled (structure, work processes, flow of information, and talent). Still, that takes you only part of the way; the rest comes via the 'hum:' that marvelous sound or feeling that tells you that the engine is running well. It's more than culture; it's reflected in the linking elements between the 'white spaces' (embedment, engagement, networks, 'hot spots', influence, and invitation).

Our diagnostic gives you a sense of where you are on the journey. For example:

A Chequered Flag

You agreed with at least 24 of the statements overall. Your mission now is to continue traveling at a consistent rate *past* the chequered flag. Take the victory lap, then gear up quickly as you approach the starting line again (since the next road is waiting to be travelled). Monitor your processes, check in regularly with your teams, consider what you are doing to annoy your employees or customers—and fix them. Consider what you are doing to delight your employees or customers and embed those actions in your journey planner.

The Yellow Flag or Caution Sign

You agreed with at least 15 of the statements overall. Next, look within the categories; where are the greatest sources of pain (disagreement) and thus, the largest potential opportunities? Is it your direction (strategy)? Or have you missed one or two elements? Is the 'hum' limited to specific projects or initiatives, or does it permeate more fully throughout the organization? Are certain individuals or teams being left behind in the race? Use this tool to monitor regularly and identify where you are 'crashing,' losing momentum or not taking the curves as tightly as you could. Use the tool to *anticipate* improvements and if the gaps persist you will be in a better (pole) position to respond.

You're going the Wrong Way!

Disagreeing with 20 or more of the statements suggests you've stalled or taken a wrong turn. More than likely, your business performance ('end-of-process') metrics have already alerted you to a problem; you're not currently meeting expectations or, perhaps, results are trending downward. It's time to regroup; make a pit stop to check all systems, processes, and information flows. Start with your strategy and describe what it means for your organization to be effective. What would it take for you to change your assessment to Agree?

Have your whole crew answer the questionnaire—your leadership team, your managers, your customers, even your external partners. Develop the new game plan with actions, responsibilities, and clear priorities to answer, "What's the right sequence to get back on track?'"

As a new CEO or senior leader, assess the organization within the first 90 days of starting your role

Engage the Board in determining the starting line

No need to reinvent the wheel – use available tools

Consider your people and the way in which the organization really operates and lives its values (unwritten rules)

Get input from all levels of the organization to get a richer picture
- Consider the relevance to the intended purpose
- Translate this feedback into enterprise-level topics

Don't hesitate to use previous audit reports. Identify the lessons learned from these assessments

Current Reality

Effective Decisions

"Research shows that enterprises fail at strategy execution because they... neglect the most important drivers of effectiveness—decision rights and information flow."[4]

In other words: how you take decisions matters. In the **Current Reality Assessment**, you learned more about that and also how information currently flows in your organization. That's useful, because it tells you who needs what data for which decisions. Perhaps that assessment also highlighted specific strengths or weaknesses in the areas of decision quality or timeliness.

We focused on effective decisions in the first section of this book, because senior executives routinely face decisions. We've also found it useful to frame opportunities and challenges as decisions. That helps you and your team to make sense of the data you gather and the insights it generates. For example, ask: What do you want to do as a result of this learning or analysis? For many of the organizations with which we've worked, decisions are not always honored. Thus, it made sense to create a tool to help senior leaders improve transparency in their decision-making and help teams to discern possible solutions, options, or choices.

We've found that all three of these things—knowing how the decision will be taken, who is participating in the decision, and accepting the decision—go a long way toward improving the effectiveness of strategy development and execution.

[4]Gary L. Neilson, Karla L. Martin, and Elizabeth Powers, "The Secrets to Successful Strategy Execution," *Harvard Business Review,* June 2008.

ROADMAP

Know what you are trying to solve and identify the decision(s) needed to solve it.

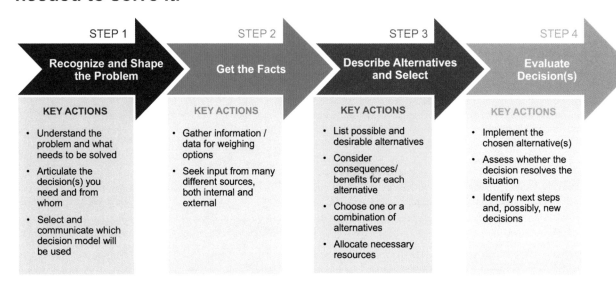

STEP 1 — **Recognize and Shape the Problem**

KEY ACTIONS

- Understand the problem and what needs to be solved
- Articulate the decision(s) you need and from whom
- Select and communicate which decision model will be used

STEP 2 — **Get the Facts**

KEY ACTIONS

- Gather information / data for weighing options
- Seek input from many different sources, both internal and external

STEP 3 — **Describe Alternatives and Select**

KEY ACTIONS

- List possible and desirable alternatives
- Consider consequences/ benefits for each alternative
- Choose one or a combination of alternatives
- Allocate necessary resources

STEP 4 — **Evaluate Decision(s)**

KEY ACTIONS

- Implement the chosen alternative(s)
- Assess whether the decision resolves the situation
- Identify next steps and, possibly, new decisions

Importantly, while decision tools and frameworks can facilitate problem resolution, decision making itself is not problem solving. It's a *process*, as you'll see in the **Effective Decisions Roadmap**. All types of decisions benefit when teams know how the decision will be made and the role of each group member in the decision-making process. Further, different situations and types of decisions call for different ways to come to a decision.

Having a clear, accepted **Decision Framework**—like in the following **Aid**—provides a common lexicon, so that everyone uses the same terms and knows what each one means. That understanding of the terms and each group member's role in making the decision reduces anxiety and misperceptions. It also helps acceptance of the decision, irrespective of whether the decision is liked.

Other decision tools reframe the opportunity or challenge so that individuals and teams can make difficult choices, particularly when there are many potentially good options. Those tools often address the tradeoffs. We particularly like matrices (and provide an **Aid** and **Examples**), because they can accommodate complex decisions.

To be clear, the process should never get in the way of actually taking and honoring decisions. At the same time, the need for speed should not circumvent a transparent, thoughtful process. It's a balance. Further, not all decisions require a multi-step process like the one shown in our **Roadmap**. Follow a common process when:

• The stakes are high.

• Uncertainty is great.

• The situation is complex.

• Multiple options are possible (and attractive).

• The nature of the decision itself is unclear.

More routine decisions likely need just a set of guidelines for who is authorized to take what types of decisions and at what levels. For example, many organizations create a simple **Authority Delegation** chart, such as the one we've provided next.

An Authority Delegation chart offers guidelines for managing more routine decisions.

Effective Decisions

		Board	CEO	CFO	Divisional VP	Functional VP	Head of Department
Delegation of Authority							
Item #	**Activity, Transaction & Decision**						
1.	**Finance**						
	1.1 Customer Credit limits			✓			
	1.2 Appointment of Financial institution		✓				
	1.3 CapEx plan	✓					
2.	**HR**						
	2.1 Recruitment of Executive Committee members		✓				
	2.2 CEO remuneration	✓					
	2.3 Appointment below Exec Committee				✓		
3.	**Sales**						
	3.1 Sales Quote						✓

Decision Framework

This Decision Framework shows four decision models – at a glance.

Model	When to Use
Autonomous Decision is made by one person without input from others	• Time for discussion is very limited • Only the decision-maker has the expertise and/or information • Clear, necessary hierarchy is in place • Broad support for the decision is not necessary
Consultative Decision is made by one person with input from others	• Time for discussion may be limited • Decision-maker has the most expertise and/or information • Clear, necessary hierarchy is in place • Broad support for the decision is not necessary • Accountability rests primarily with the decision-maker
Majority Decision is made by the group by assessing which choice is favored by most of the members—usually by taking a vote; those who do not favor the choice may or may not agree to support the decision	• Time for discussion is limited • Hierarchy is not in place, or not important • Broad support for the decision is not necessary • Opinion is clearly split • Middle ground is difficult to find
Consensus All feel that they have had a voice. All agree to support the decision, even if it goes against their opinion (NOT unanimous)	• Ample time is available for discussion • Broad support for the decision is critical to the mission

Be explicit about which decision model you are using for each decision.

Effective Decisions

 AID

A matrix is a decision tool to consider the relative value of multiple ideas, solutions, options, approaches, etc.

Frame and Use the Matrix Systematically	Example of Questions
1. List ideas, solutions, options, approaches to consider (labeled as a,b,c on the matrix) 2. Define axes carefully: write 3 or 5 questions for each axis with binary (Yes/No) answers to avoid consistently landing in the middle 3. Use ball size to add a third dimension, if desired (e.g., strategic importance, capital investment, readiness to act)	**Impact for our client:** • To what extent do our current projects and initiatives fit? • What new things will we do? • In what order should we do them? • Which enablers most enhance the success of our focus areas? **Level of effort for us:** • What will it take to move a *Monitor/Improve* item into focus ? Is it worth it? • We can't do it all. What will we let go? • Who needs to be involved— including those who will monitor low effort, higher potential impact items? • What are the implications for other parts of the company?

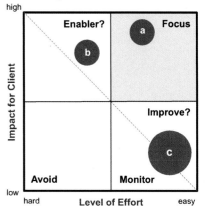

Impact vs. Level of Effort

Tip:

Meaning comes from the conversation as you decide where to place each option, opportunity, solution, etc.

Tips:
• *Ground decisions in data wherever possible, yet embrace the inherent uncertainty*
• *Focus on relativity—often you're choosing among many things that are all attractive or useful. Typically, we simply can't do everything!*

Compare the risk assessment profile of various projects using two matrices to support your investment decision.

Step 1:
Read projects on first matrix (Risk vs. Strategic Fit) with bubble size linked to total investment.

Step 2:
Read projects on second matrix (Risk vs. Financial Assessment) with bubble size linked to total investment.

High risk

Overall risk assessment

Project 3= $7M

Project 1 = $25M

Project 4= $3M

Project 2 = $30M

Low risk

Lower strategic impact — Overall strategic fit — Higher strategic impact

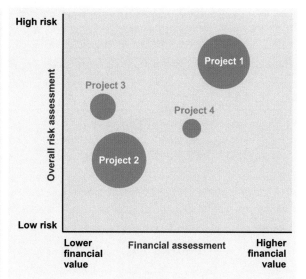

High risk

Overall risk assessment

Project 3

Project 1

Project 4

Project 2

Low risk

Lower financial value — Financial assessment — Higher financial value

It is easier to draw conclusions using visuals, for example:

Project 1 ✓ *(GO)*   ***Project 2*** ✗ *(No GO)*   ***Project 3*** ✗ *(No GO)*   ***Project 4*** ✓ *(GO with lower priority)*

Effective Decisions

Ground decisions in facts and data. Intuition aids analysis and interpretation.

Don't skip steps, thinking they will take too much time or cost too much.

- The more complex the decision, the more important it is to follow through

Think creatively and positively to describe potential alternatives.

Prioritize alternatives, options, ideas solutions, etc., using common criteria.

- Incorporate your company values
- Consider pros and cons for each alternative, plus potential mitigation steps or implications for other parts of the company or business

Don't stay isolated even if it is an autonomous decision.

Conflict is a natural part of the process.

- The key is how you use conflict to further your group work

Effective Decisions

Onboarding

Much has been written about the benefits of onboarding, particularly for new hires. Done well, onboarding makes good business sense, as it gets people up to speed quickly, builds trust, and, ultimately, reduces turnover. It capitalizes on the new employee's enthusiasm about joining the company, which generally enhances a willingness to learn. Taking time up front to help new staff understand the rules of the road integrates them more rapidly into the company and instills a sense of your culture, values, and ways of working. Those efforts demonstrate commitment to developing your people and make it easier for them to be successful, more quickly. In return, you get enhanced effectiveness, reduced time-to-contribution, and improved retention—all of which decrease the cost of talent acquisition.

ROADMAP

A relatively simple onboarding process: Focus on early planning, consistent action, and follow-up.

STEP 1	STEP 2	STEP 3	STEP 4
Define Objectives	**Identify Learning Agenda and Select Tools**	**Engage the Organization**	**Monitor Progress**

KEY ACTIONS

- Agree on overarching business goals: what you hope to achieve
- Define success for the program
- Set objectives for specific roles and the team, as needed

KEY ACTIONS

- Identify what the leader must know and do, with timeframes
- Choose or create tools to enable that learning
- Determine the appropriate mix of interactive and self-directed learning
- Set the timeline for each phase of onboarding

KEY ACTIONS

- Share the program with the team and the organization
- Agree who does what, by when
- Get feedback from the organization
- Agree on timelines for ongoing communication, as needed

KEY ACTIONS

- Identify metrics (e.g., employee retention at 6, 12 months)
- Establish the baseline—where are you now?
- Set timeline for review—it takes time to see results
- Identify lessons learned to refresh program at least annually

In our experience, however, it is less common for CEOs or their companies to onboard existing staff members when these people first become senior managers or join the leadership team. Because a leader already has a history with the organization, others naturally assume that he or she automatically knows how things work and what it takes to be successful. To some extent that is true. These individuals likely have a good understanding of the culture and values, and they have successfully navigated the organization to land this new role.

 AID

Best Practices for Onboarding

Do these six things well for effective onboarding.

1. Start the process prior to Day 1
2. Address administrative tasks in advance
3. Involve the senior leader
4. Involve business leaders – don't leave this to the human resources team
5. Develop formal and individualized plans
6. Track plans and program's progress against specific metrics, over time

Look beyond tactical elements. Focus on what's needed to integrate the leader into the team and/or organization.

On the other hand, the new leader may not know the nuances of working with the leadership team. Further, the addition of a new leader typically changes how the team works, simply by virtue of their presence on the team. That's not necessarily a bad thing. It's also why we felt it was important to include the **Onboarding Tool**. Effectively onboarding new members of the leadership team (or management) increases the effectiveness of the entire team, not just individual leaders.

Our **Onboarding Checklist Aid** covers the full cycle of onboarding, beginning during the hiring process (for both internal and external hires) and concluding with the first mid-year and annual reviews. It connects talent acquisition, development, and management, smoothing the transition from prospective to seasoned staff member. A checklist is handy in that it creates a simple way to manage the details over time, streamline the process, and enhance consistency across the organization. Start by identifying specific audiences (e.g., new hire, new leader, new manager), then defining success for that audience. Adapt the **Onboarding Checklist** to suit the needs of each audience. For example, new hires (at any level) need information about company culture, benefits, and fundamental systems. First time members of management or the leadership team require more attention to the way things work in their new team and how they best contribute.

Define success for your onboarding program.

Leaders Develop	Company Obtains
• Shared understanding of the business objectives—and this leader's role in achieving them • Clear understanding of what is expected, from whom, by when • Knowledge of the 'secret handshakes' that bind the leadership team • Support system and network to find information, share experiences, and navigate the organization and team effectively • Deeper connection and less stress for the new leader	• Increased employee retention among senior leadership • More diverse leadership team • Reduced turnover costs, especially among senior leaders • Clear sense of direction and stronger execution by leaders' direct reports • Greater sense of connection and satisfaction among entire leadership team • Cohesive team that works together well

Onboarding increases the effectiveness of the entire leadership team, not just individual leaders.

Onboarding

AID

Use a checklist to manage the details and streamline the process.

Before Hiring Process Starts	Responsibility	Status*
Share information about your company, its culture, and values on public-facing media, (e.g., website, social media pages, employee testimonials, recruiting materials)	HR and talent acquisition team	

4-6 Weeks Prior to First Day	Responsibility	Status*
Send welcome email (or letter) and provide access to internal employee portal	HR operations team	
Send employee handbook and all new-hire forms to be completed and returned by specific deadline	HR operations team	
Provide specific, written directions for employee to report (location, time, parking, point of contact, etc.)	HR business partner and operations team	
Send "First Day" and "First Week" itinerary/agenda, including meetings with N+1 and N+2	HR business partner	
Prepare employee work area including computer, phone, business cards, supplies	HR business partner and hiring manager	

On the First Day	Responsibility	Status*
Lay the foundation: basic activities such as phones, computers, intranet, parking, facilities layout, etc.	Point of contact	
Review company vision, mission, and values; relate these to new leader's role	Hiring manager	
Introduce new leader to their internal peer mentor	Hiring manager	
Welcome new leader and introduce them to team members	Hiring manager	

*Use a traffic light to measure status:
● **Not Started (or not ready)** ○ **Stalled (or moving slowly)** ● **Full Throttle (or all set, completed)**

Onboarding

During the First Week	Responsibility	Status*
Introduce new leader to key staff, managers, and peers	Hiring manager and peer mentor	
Clarify expectations and set short term goals with N+1, N+2 separately *(leader schedules similar meetings with direct reports);* explain key business processes and authorization matrix	Hiring manager (or N+1) and N+2	
Engage new leader in specific tasks, meetings, and work to build internal knowledge and speed integration	Hiring manager	

The First 90 Days	Responsibility	Status*
Encourage exploration of, learning about, and connections to the organization via site tours, invitations to key meetings, participation in company events, etc.	Hiring manager and peer mentor	
Check in regularly with new leader—track progress vs. short-term goals, challenges, questions, resource needs, etc.	Hiring manager	
Introduce new leader to broader network of peers, staff, and knowledge experts across the organization	Hiring manager and peer mentor	
Monitor peer mentoring relationship and its effectiveness	Hiring manager and HR business partner	
Solicit feedback from new leader regarding onboarding experience	HR business partner	

The First Mid-Year and Annual Reviews	Responsibility	Status*
Solicit feedback, including relationships, connections, and expectations	Hiring manager and peer mentor	
Evaluate progress toward goals and set new goals with N+1, N+2 separately *(leader schedules similar meetings with direct reports)*	Hiring manager (or N+1), N+2 and new leader	
Set up a collaborative individual development plan to continue learning and growing within the organization	Hiring manager and new leader	

Onboarding

ACCELERATION TIPS

Divide onboarding activities into categories.
- Getting in the door: HR information/processes
- Setting up: Tools and equipment
- Knowing the organization: Culture, values, ways of working
- Learning the role and the team
- Building network of contacts

Engage the new leader's peers in the process—deliberately and explicitly.
- Identify a specific peer partner or mentor to help new leader acclimate
- Ask all peers to introduce the leader to others and help create new network

Encourage specific meet ups, including learning or listening 'tours' to experience the breadth and depth of the organization and how it works.

Create opportunities for feedback and shared learning.
- Offer tools for journaling the experience or learning
- Set specific timeline for check-in and review

Onboarding

Section 2: Plan the Journey

You've set the destination and have a good sense of where you're headed. You know your starting point and what you might encounter along the way. Ideally, your team shares your passion for reaching the destination successfully.

Planning the journey is about defining the path you'll take to reach the destination. It's all about the 'how'—what routes, decisions, equipment, skills, and people you will need to close the gap between your current reality and the desired position. Most journey plans also include key milestones that give you both targets to aim for and a sense of progress.

> **Planning the journey includes linking high-level strategic priorities with the specific actions needed at the operational level.**

Navigational tools, including electronic global positioning systems (GPS), help to calculate the route, while showing the other vehicles, landmarks, and hazards on the road. A GPS also offers multiple vantage points from which to view the route. That's useful for strategic planning. At the highest level, you decide where to focus and identify the critical few things that you'll do to reach the destination—your company's strategic priorities. That's the 30,000 foot or company level. Zoom in to see how each part of the business comes together to help the company reach the destination. That's the operating level.

Planning the journey includes linking high-level strategic priorities with the specific actions needed at the operational level. Here are some questions to consider as you make that link and plan the journey:

Questions to Consider:

- **Who do we consider to be our competitors today? Who might emerge during our planning timeframe? What is their implied strategy?**
- **Have we matched what we sell to what our customers need or want?**
- **On what will we focus? What gaps are most critical to address?**
- **How (and when) will we close the critical gaps?**
- **What capabilities, resources, equipment, and capital investment do we need? How and when will we get them?**
- **Do we have a systematic way to identify and manage our exposure to potential risks?**
- **How frequently will we review and assess potential risks and our progress toward the objectives?**
- **How does each functional area contribute to company priorities? What will each line of business, business unit, or product group do to contribute?**

How to use the Tools to Plan the Journey:

The tools in this section help you lay out your strategy—to define explicitly the ways in which you close the gaps between your current position and the vision you've set for your business. Use the **Competitive Positioning Tool** to determine where you stand versus your competitors, highlighting their implied strategies, and anticipating where they may challenge you.

Once you know where you stand, the **Value Propositions Tool** can help clarify the value you offer to customers overall and for each product/service. The **Gap Analysis Tool** builds on your prior understanding of the **External Landscape**, **Current Reality**, and **Competitive Positioning**. The Tool includes a framework for identifying the critical factors needed to succeed in achieving your vision (and at what level of proficiency) and how well you currently perform on those factors, relative to what's needed. Consequently, the results of your gap analysis inform your strategic focus; it's the culmination of extensive learning about your context, capabilities, and customers.

> **Regular strategic and operational review is a key part of actively balancing strategy and operations, especially as your landscape changes.**

Strategy is the set of decisions and actions that get you where you want to go. It's much easier to do that based on a few critical focus areas which you identify using the **Strategic Planning Tool**. Create a **Strategic Dashboard** to highlight those focus areas and the intervals at which you will measure progress along the way. That not only raises

the visibility of the strategic elements, but it also shows how operating activities must contribute to each of the strategic objectives.

Regular strategic and operational review is a key part of actively balancing strategy and operations, especially as your landscape changes.

Typically, closing the gaps requires additional or different capital resources, and mitigating risks. The **Capital Investment Visibility Tool** provides tips and examples to create value by planning and monitoring capital investment. The **Risk Assessment Tool** guides you in assessing your exposure to potential risks and establishing practices to mitigate them.

Regular strategic and operational review is a key part of actively balancing strategy and operations, especially as your landscape changes. As you measure progress in reaching the milestones you've identified, consider also whether it's time to shift resources or emphasis, or to detour from the original path.

Tools

Competitive Positioning	Strategic Dashboard
Value Propositions	Capital Investment Visibility
Gap Analysis	Risk Assessment
Strategic Planning	

Competitive Positioning

Much has been written about the importance of understanding where you fit versus the competition. Michael Porter's *Competitive Strategy* is among the most well-known books about why it's important to take a careful, multi-faceted look at your competitors as you shape strategy. Moreover, Porter's Five Forces model focuses on the microeconomic forces that are closest to the company and describe competitive intensity in the company's *industry*.[2] That intensity dramatically impacts the ability of your company to profitably serve its customers. For nonprofit organizations, the analysis helps define how easy or hard it may be to raise money, secure members, or otherwise attract new contributors to critical programs or services you offer.

Earlier, we mentioned Porter's Five Forces model among the resources you may wish to tap in assessing your **Current Reality**. It gives you a quick snapshot of where you are at any given moment, and as you consider the industry as a whole—or how the collective actions of competitors impact your strategic position. In the **Competitive Positioning Tool**, we help you dive more deeply into individual competitors. Why? Because your competitors' behaviors impact your own decisions and actions. They are a key contributor to traffic—or the intensity of competition—in your market. Actively and regularly review competitors to better anticipate shifts in competitors' behaviors and make decisions about how you'll adjust your own position. For example, you may see a big opportunity to acquire or merge with a competitor. Or, a competitor's behavior may signal a shift in the industry or an emerging disruptor. The earlier you recognize this, the better able you are to respond.

[1]Michael E. Porter, *Competitive Strategy*, (New York: Free Press, 1980).

[2]Ibid.

Know current competitors and who (or what) to monitor.

Competitive Positioning

STEP 1	STEP 2	STEP 3
Describe the Players	**Assess your Position**	**Set your Watch List and Timeline**

KEY ACTIONS

- Identify and characterize competitors
- List the most important characteristics for any player in your business
- Describe competitors against the common characteristics

KEY ACTIONS

- Agree on the top competitors in each category
- Evaluate your business vs. key players with the same characteristics
- Determine the relative position of each competitor and your company
- Highlight implications: potential threats, opportunities, unmet customer needs, partners, etc.

KEY ACTIONS

- Agree on most critical factors or elements to monitor—and why
- Identify the top 5-10 competitors to track more closely
- Incorporate formal, periodic competitive review into your management timeline

The **Competitive Positioning Roadmap** guides you through a process to describe the players and your position relative to them, then to establish a framework to monitor changes over time. Competitors come and go in any industry, and often appear from unexpected areas. Thus, not only must you know today's competitors well, but you should know who (or what) to watch as things change. Incorporate regular competitive reviews into your management cycle. Focus on the possible implications of your competitive position at these periodic intervals.

As you can see from the **Competitive Positioning—Key Resources Aid**, other tools and resources provide additional lenses through which to consider your positioning in a much more granular way. Use these and other tools to gather intelligence about your competitors and develop insights about the market and where you stand. That understanding becomes a critical contributor to **Gap Analysis** and setting strategic priorities.

> **Successive analyses build competitive intelligence across your whole team.**

Successive analyses build competitive intelligence across your whole team. These help you to focus on trends, identify implications, and consider the extent to which you are keeping up with—or passing by—your competition. We've included several **Examples** and **Aids** to guide you. As you execute your strategy, return to this tool regularly so that you maintain an ongoing understanding of your position.

AID

Competitive Positioning—Key Resources

Incorporate existing resources, data, and tools for analyzing competitors into your approach.

Purpose or Step	Resources or Frameworks
Describing the key players	Analyst reports (public companies); internet search; website and social media presence
Assessing your position	Survey or comparative charts; benchmarking data
Considering the implications	Numerous charts, graphs, visuals exist online (e.g., search competitive analysis, competitive positioning, or competitive landscape templates)

AID

Competitive Analysis

At regular intervals, re-consider your competitive position and possible implications.

1 Scan positioning of competitors, vendors, partners

- Who is competing today? Who could be the new entrants? By when?
- Which partners may become competitors? Which competitors might partner?
- How frequently and easily do competitors enter or exit?
- Where do you fit? Are you ahead of, alongside, or behind the competition?

2 Look for trends

- When taking multiple snapshots of your competitive position over time, can you identify trends?
- What new opportunities or threats are emerging?
- To what extent is it becoming easier or harder to maintain your pace?

3 Adapt strategic decisions and actions as needed

- Has the competition become more or less intense?
- What alternate strategies can you develop? What tactics will you deploy?
- How do you shift the competitive field?
- Who's coming up from behind?
- What will it take to create a leadership position?
- Must you lead or is it better to follow quickly?

Competitive Positioning

Competitive Analysis — Performance

Compare your business performance to competitors using a common set of critical factors for your target market and a common framework.

Competitive Market

Competitive Market		Data Sources	Person Responsible	Competitor 1	Competitor 2	Competitor 3	Competitor 4
Relevant Market Data	Target Market						
	Market Share						
	Projected Growth						
	Marketing approach / position						
Relevant Product Data	Breadth of Products & Services (broad, deep, limited)						
	Average Sales Growth (last 5 yrs)						
	Pricing						
Operating	Distribution Channels						
	Manufacturing Capacity						
	Geographic coverage / locations						
Financial	Estimated Margin						
	Debt Equity						
	Key Revenue Streams						
Workforce	Access to skilled, technical labor						
Strategic Signals	Perceived or stated business strategy						
	Key partners						
	Speed / approach to bringing new products to market						

Source: Strategy for Real © 2018. Used with permission.

Competitive Positioning

Competitive Analysis — Trends

Focus on trends, implications, and relative positioning or results to help synthesize data.

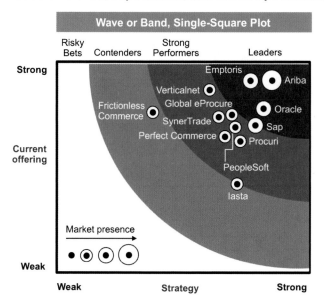

Wave or Band, Single-Square Plot

Useful for diving into specific elements of competitive position—e.g., market position, business scale, revenue or pricing. Create separate charts for each focus area.

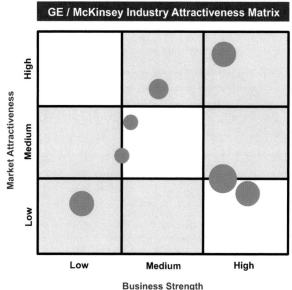

GE / McKinsey Industry Attractiveness Matrix

Originally designed to assess business units. Helpful when considering market entry/exit, or opportunities to reposition product lines, brand, organization.

Source: Paul Seibert. Hubtechinsider.wordpress.com. 2011.

Competitive Positioning

Competitive Landscape Map

Designed for companies with a diverse product offering who compete with many different company types.

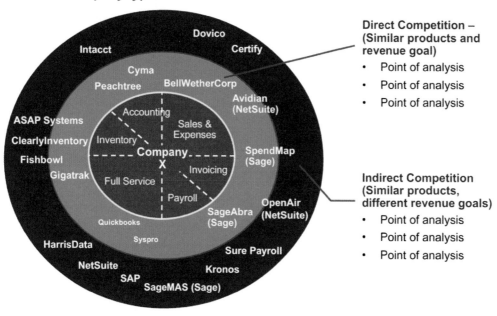

**Direct Competition –
(Similar products and
revenue goal)**

- Point of analysis
- Point of analysis
- Point of analysis

**Indirect Competition
(Similar products,
different revenue goals)**

- Point of analysis
- Point of analysis
- Point of analysis

Source: Daniel Burstein, MECLABS Competitive Analysis Presentation Template

AID

Types of Competitors

Category of Competitor	What to Do
1. Direct or Primary Targeting the same audience, offering the same products	*Action:* Keep on your radar at all time They make money from the same thing you do; your sales team will go head-to-head with theirs
2. Adjacent or Secondary Offering a high-or-low-end version or similar product for different audience	*Action:* Consider them as an opportunity; watch and potentially go after them They don't drive revenue the same way you do Content marketing can be a powerful tool
3. Tangential Related, trending, or along your value chain	*Action:* Anticipate their movements; keep ears and eyes open in the marketplace to always understand customers needs They use the same resources they could have committed to your products

Competitive Positioning

AID

Competitor Watch List

Develop your Competitor Watch list

Step 1: List most important competitors and their types

Step 2: Identify key flags: things that most impact your business or position (positively or negatively)

Step 3: Assign accountability for maintaining competitive intelligence

Step 4: Set timeline for updating and sharing competitive data and analysis

Top Competitors in your Space				Things to Watch for				
Competitor Name	M&A Deal	Quarterly	Market Share	Monthly	Profitability	Quarterly	New Product	Monthly
WWW			-1%				No	
XXX			5%	⚑	+20$M	⚑	Yes	⚑
YYY			0%				No	
ZZZ			-4%				No	

Tips:

- *Assign responsibility for actively monitoring and evaluating competitive positions*
- *Choose or adapt a framework to best suit your situation*

Successive analyses build competitive intelligence across your team.

Data is key: Use objective metrics from reliable sources to substantiate the analysis and perceived implications.

A common framework for gathering data and tracking changes over time eases comparison across competitors.
- Assign specific responsibility and adjust the watch list as needed

Make it visual: Graphs and charts encourage analysis and thinking about the big picture, rather than the details.
- Focus on the implications and begin framing decisions about what actions you will take
- It's relative, rather than absolute—that's a judgment call, based on data and your understanding

Over time, highlight shifts and changes among and within competitors.
- Anticipate and take proactive steps to mitigate risk or capitalize on an opportunity

Competitive Positioning

Value Propositions

A value proposition tells target customers what to expect from your product or service. More than simply a statement of value (as its name suggests), it's a promise made to your customers about the nature of the benefit you offer and, specifically, to whom. The best value proposition statements are easily read and immediately visible on all customer facing materials.

ROADMAP

Build on deep knowledge of customers and your products/services to write and test your value proposition.

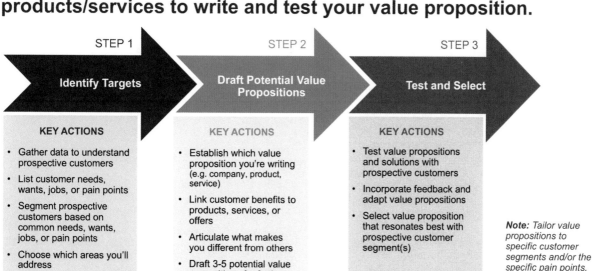

STEP 1 — Identify Targets

STEP 2 — Draft Potential Value Propositions

STEP 3 — Test and Select

KEY ACTIONS

- Gather data to understand prospective customers
- List customer needs, wants, jobs, or pain points
- Segment prospective customers based on common needs, wants, jobs, or pain points
- Choose which areas you'll address

KEY ACTIONS

- Establish which value proposition you're writing (e.g. company, product, service)
- Link customer benefits to products, services, or offers
- Articulate what makes you different from others
- Draft 3-5 potential value propositions for further testing

KEY ACTIONS

- Test value propositions and solutions with prospective customers
- Incorporate feedback and adapt value propositions
- Select value proposition that resonates best with prospective customer segment(s)

Note: Tailor value propositions to specific customer segments and/or the specific pain points, wants, needs, or jobs you address via your product or service

While the statement itself should be quite simple, a good value proposition is relatively complex and incredibly useful. It makes the connection between a customer segment's needs (usually expressed as a pain, gain, or job they need to do), and the way in which your product or service satisfies that need. Use the **Value Propositions Tool** to gain insight into your customers and articulate the value of your product or service. Working through the process outlined in the **Value Proposition Roadmap** will tell you what you do and do not know about your customers' needs, and in what ways you meet these needs or help them to do their jobs. Equally important, thinking about your customers in this structured way encourages deeper understanding of their perspective. That external perspective prevents myopia and rightfully returns your focus to your customers. Their perceptions of your products and services are your reality—regardless of whether or not you agree.

Before you start, be sure everyone has the same understanding of what you mean by customer pains, gains, and jobs. On the surface, these definitions may seem straightforward. Yet, our experience—and that of other marketing experts—suggests not everyone interprets these in the same way.[3] That can result in missed opportunities or statements of value that are more about your perspective than that of your customers. We've included our definition and factors to consider in the following table.

[3]See also: Clayton M. Christensen, Taddy Hall, Karen Dillon, and David S. Duncan, "Know Your Customers' Jobs to Be Done," *Harvard Business Review*, September 2016, and Alex Osterwalder, Yves Pigneur, Greg Bernarda, and Alan Smith, *Value Proposition Design* (New York: Wiley, 2014).

Clarify Your Terms

Pain	Gain	Job
Specific to each customer segment and significantly dependent upon circumstances, importance of each pain, gain, or job lies solely in the mind of the customer.		

	Pain	Gain	Job
Answers the questions	What risks or obstacles do customers face? What negative consequences or results do they encounter?	What outcomes do our customers want to achieve? What benefits do they seek?	What are customers trying to get done in their work/lives? What problems are they trying to solve? What needs do they want to satisfy?
Often means this	Pains stem from inadequate or no solutions or undesired characteristics	Gains make things easier or delight customers	A job is often the experience they want to create – for themselves, others, or customers
Includes these elements	• Risks are the customer's unwanted possible consequences or results; things they want to avoid • Obstacles include things that make it harder for customers to do their jobs or get the outcomes they seek • Negative consequences include what doesn't work, causes mistakes, feels bad, or isn't pleasing to the customer	• Required gains make the solution work: **Got to Have** • Desired gains are attributes, improvements, savings, or features that exceed customer expectations: **Nice to Have** • Unexpected gains delight customers, often solving a problem or meeting a need they didn't know they had: **Love Having**	• Functional jobs relate to task completion or problem solving • Social jobs deal with how a customer wants to be perceived or seen by others • Emotional jobs evoke feelings about the outcomes (e.g., security, less stress, valued)

Value Propositions

Often, your value proposition also describes what makes your product or service distinct from what your competitors do or provide. That's where the **Competitive Positioning Tool** may help. Build on that characterization of your competitors to set your product or service apart from others. For example, you may see an opportunity to launch a new product feature based on your competitor's reviews. Your feature may solve a stated problem, relieve a pain, or help prospective customers do something that your competitors don't do.

Uber started in a similar way. When Uber launched in San Francisco in 2009, it offered a much-needed alternative to the city's fractured transportation system. After Travis Kalanick and Garrett Camp couldn't hail a cab one snowy evening in Paris, they came up with the idea for an app that would allow them to book a ride with the tap of a button.

Add in what you've learned from independent reviews of your products and services. Do not shy away from the negatives; they reflect customer experience and perception. And their perception is what you must address.

Numerous frameworks already exist to help you in assessing customer needs and comparing your products and services to that of competitors. They can be terrific resources both to jump-start your analysis and to add an independent, objective assessment. We've assembled a **Key Resources Aid** listing how you might use some of the more common resources to construct your value propositions. For the most part, these resources focus on gathering the data to enhance or affirm your understanding of your customers and how they (and others) view your products and services.

> **The best and most compelling value propositions highlight customer benefits from the perspective of the customer.**

Most companies or organizations have created a statement describing the value or intended benefit of their product or services. Yet, not all such statements are created equal. The best and most compelling value propositions highlight customer benefits from the perspective of the customer—reflecting what the customer gets from the product or service. Strong value propositions are simple and fact-based. After all, it's easy for the prospective customer to verify your statements. The following **Aid** summarizes what makes a good value proposition.

It cannot be overstated: your value proposition is customer-facing. It should speak directly to your current and prospective customers, so that *they* see themselves and their organizations benefiting directly from what you do. Our **Aids** and **Examples** show the way.

Once you've defined and tested your value proposition, take a look at the business model that will accompany it. Doing so will help you to connect the external, customer view with the internal elements—operations, pricing, service delivery—in a profitable way. This is key to accelerating progress.

Value Propositions

 AID

What Makes a Good Value Proposition

A Good Value Proposition is:

Highly targeted and specific.
- Most companies need multiple value propositions—one for each combination of product/service and customer segment

Focused on the *benefit* to customers, not the features or deliverable (what you do).
- This lets you see what your customers think of you and your products/services

Unique to you, in the minds of your customer.
- Customers expect many things; doing them is necessary but won't persuade a customer to buy from you versus someone else
- Value propositions include *perceived* value, not just actual value; be better than everyone else *in the minds of your customer*

Embedded in your brand and at the core of its messaging.

Equally clear internally and externally.
- **Internally:** Helps you shape decisions, does the new feature further our value proposition for customers? If not, move on
- **Externally:** Lets customers know immediately what to expect and the fact-based reasons they should do what you want them to do (buy, subscribe, visit, sell, etc.)

The connection between your customer's goals and how your product helps to meet them.

 AID

Value Propositions – Key Resources

Don't reinvent the wheel. Use the combination of tools that works best for you.

Purpose or Step	Tools & Resources
Competitive positioning	Independent rankings, testing, or summaries of customer reviews of similar products (e.g., *Consumer Reports* polls or reviews)
Assessing customer needs or wants	Customer surveys, focus groups, independent polls, market research, etc.
Mapping products or services to customer needs, wants, concerns[4]	Feature-Advantage-Benefit (FAB) process Strategyzer's *Value Proposition Design*
Writing a value proposition[5]	Strategyzer's *Value Proposition Design*. See also *Business Model Generation*
Testing value propositions	Customer journey maps, focus groups, pilot programs, prototyping

Sources: Alex Osterwalder, Yves Pigneur, Gregory Bernarda, and Alan Smith. *Value Proposition Design* (Wiley, 2014); Alex Osterwalder and Yves Pigneur. *Business Model Generation* (2010).

Value Propositions

 AID

How to Create a Value Proposition

A four-step approach to creating a value proposition.

Step 1: Create Customer Profiles

Understand customer segments

- Identify customer pains
- Identify customer gains
- Analyze jobs your customers need done

Tip: Rank each set of pains, gains, and jobs to focus on the most important and impactful from the customer perceptive

Step 3

Match value map to customer profiles to create possible value propositions

Step 2: Create Value Map

Characterize products and services offered to customers

- Identify those that relieve customer pains
- Identify those that create customer gains
- Describe jobs you may do for customers

Step 4: Test Value Propositions with prospective customers and select

Value Propositions

AID

Customer and Value Questions

Questions to guide your customer profiles and value map.

Key Questions – Customer Profile	Key Questions – Value Map
• What types of customers (or segments) might we serve?	• What perceived value do we offer? (e.g., our customers rave about…)
• Who benefits most if we satisfy the need or resolve the pain?	• In what ways and how well do we meet customer needs and wants, or help them do their jobs?
• What do we know about the customers' wants, needs, pain points, or jobs?	• What features of our solution (product or service) will produce the desired outcomes for prospective customers?
• What specific outcomes do prospective customer segments want?	• What business/economic benefits will the prospective customer get for achieving these outcomes?
• How does each customer segment identify success?	• What are the significant reasons for purchasing a product or service like ours?
	• What do we do or offer that makes us better than the competition in delivering this value?

Value Propositions

Examples of Value Propositions

Uber	Uber is the smartest way to get around. One tap and a car comes directly to you. Your driver knows where to go. And payment is completely cashless.
Unbounce	Build, publish, and test landing pages without any IT support.
Square	Start accepting credit cards today. Sign up and we'll mail you a free Square Card Reader. (followed by clear, bulleted list of benefits).
Mailchimp	Send better email.
Bitly	Shorten. Share. Measure. Join Bitly, the world's leading link management platform.

Value Propositions

Clearly define your business model.

A strong value proposition can get you in the door and close the sale.
- It's insufficient on its own. Support it with a clear business model
- Your perceived and actual brand should reflect your value proposition—you are known for both

Your business model describes how you will deliver on your promised value.
- Largely internally-facing, it includes the external partners or relationships that are critically important to deliver value
- A single business model often encompasses multiple products/services and customer segments

A business model is <u>not</u> the same as pricing.
- Revenue, cost, and profit are all important—but only part of the equation
- Your business model specifies the key resources, capabilities, channels, and activities needed across multiple value propositions—each serving a specific customer segment

Gap Analysis

Before identifying the decisions and actions you will take to achieve your vision, it's useful to understand both what's needed to be successful and how you perform versus what the market requires. That difference—between your level of proficiency and what's required—describes the nature of the gap between where you are now and where you want to be.

If you accessed the tools sequentially, **Gap Analysis** brings together much of what you've done to date, using a variety of other tools: **External Landscape**, **Current Reality**, **Competitive Positioning**, and **Value Propositions**. If you've jumped into the book here, you will need a deep, shared understanding of your external environment, competitors, customers, internal capabilities, and the value you offer. This tool helps you put that understanding into a framework that aids focus—and forms the foundation of your strategic plan.

ROADMAP

Build on what you've already learned to identify the most critical and relevant gaps.

Gap Analysis

STEP 1	STEP 2	STEP 3
Identify Critical Capabilities	**Assess Proficiency**	**Highlight Critical Gaps**

KEY ACTIONS

- Consider implications of competitive and market analysis, customer assessment, and value propositions
- Select 3-5 potential areas for further investigation
- Identify the capabilities required for success in each potential area
  - Should be externally-facing: what do the market and customers say?
- Evaluate your core competences
  - Identify distinguishing competitive advantage, if applicable.

KEY ACTIONS

- Define the level of proficiency required in each capability
  - Which are needed to play or simply be in that market?
  - Which capabilities let you compete vs. others?
  - Which are winning or leading capabilities that set you apart from most others?
- Assess your proficiency vs. market requirements and the competition

KEY ACTIONS

- Identify gaps between market requirements and your proficiency
  - Look for themes and broader implications
  - Not everything must be done at the "win" level
- Consider which are most important for growth
  - Do you have all the 'play' capabilities to pursue new markets or customer segments?
  - What capabilities will you enhance to expand markets?
  - What areas of strength can be used to mitigate weaknesses?
- Describe critical gaps

Your gap analysis is also a blend of internal and external perspectives. As we often suggest, start externally. In the first step, the **Gap Analysis Roadmap** directs you to consider what your markets and customers say. Then build on data and insights you've already assembled to suggest potential areas for further investigation as strategic opportunities. Those insights also provide a picture of what's needed and at what level of proficiency. The gap is determined by how well you perform vs. what the market requires. Look for the areas that are most relevant to or impactful for your business and objectives.

You don't have to be excellent at everything—nor should you be. On the other hand, there are some fundamental things you've got to do or have, just to be allowed to participate in that market. For example, in today's world, a data center player must have the ability to deliver security and reliable power to customers. Those that do that within a short time after the customer's initial inquiry win more contracts. And that beats the competition and speeds growth.

A gap analysis can also help you identify areas to avoid or determine how to shift resources in favor of higher-impact investments. Again, you don't have to be exceptional at everything. What does the market require? How well do you deliver?

 AID

How to Conduct A Gap Analysis

Step 1: Identify critical capabilities to achieve vision.

Identify capabilities and resources most important to achieve your vision.

- Consider all prior analyses: external context, internal capabilities
- Incorporate lessons learned from prior business results and current competitive positioning
- Include both external perspectives and internal assessments
- Think about each core business areas separately

Step 2: Drill down into the level of proficiency required for success.

What level of proficiency for **each** critical capability is required?

- *Play* = capability needed to play in this area; all must have to cross threshold
- *Compete* = capability required to be competitive and to keep pace with others
- *Win* = capability can be distinguishing; few others do this well or consistently

Step 4: GAP 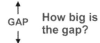 **Identify gaps: difference between what's required for success and where you are today** GAP How big is the gap?

Step 3: Assess your level of proficiency for each critical capability.

What is **your** level of proficiency in each critical capability?

- Bear in mind your assessment of strengths and weaknesses
- Identify those that are potential core competencies

Tip: Focus on your core business areas.   Sources: Adapted from Strategy for Real; Used with permission.

Gap Analysis

Gap Analysis Results

Compare required and actual proficiency to reveal gaps.

Critical Capabilities	Required Proficiency*	Our Proficiency*	Comments
Using technology effectively to address participant's needs	P	P	
Good partners in providing info for/to hub	P	n/a	
Catalyst for users & audiences to come together	P	P	
Ability to think "we + others;" assume/play variety of roles with partners (e.g., lead, cooperative, one of many, etc.)	P	n/a	
Keen management of brand	P	P	
Ability to think & act in terns of 'connecting' vs. being 'the sole or key source'	C	P	
Openness, willingness, and ability to relinquish some control	P	n/a	Very different mental model for us
Ability to sift data/info so that it's meaningful	W	W	Likely core competence
Ability to welcome, incorporate, and channel a variety of ideas	P	n/a	
Deep knowledge of our 3 markets	C	C	Only know 2 markets really well

Implications

We can exploit a core competence to be successful as an 'information hub.'

Focus on adding partners, and adjusting our mental model and approach to new ideas and our role.

Proficiency Legend
P = Play   C = Compete   W = Win

Sources: Adapted from Strategy for Real; Used with permission.

Gap Analysis

Don't start from scratch.

Build on all you've learned to date.
- Your gap analysis encompasses both the external perspective and your internal knowledge
- Add competitive and customer intelligence to test your assumptions about how good you are

Look at the gap analysis as a puzzle: What pieces are missing? Which ones don't fit securely?

Avoid diving too deeply.
- Focus on the enterprise level and key opportunities you might pursue in reaching your vision
- Be sufficiently specific to aid understanding with broad themes that synthesize your thinking

Gap Analysis

Strategic Planning

No doubt many of you jumped immediately to this tool. After all, what's a book about aligning strategy and operations without a **Strategic Planning Tool**.

If you're one of those people, welcome. In many ways, constructing your strategy is fairly simple—as you'll see in the **Strategic Planning Roadmap**. In other ways, it's quite complex and certainly, a comprehensive effort. Strategic planning is the result of myriad, varied insights and thinking. It's grounded in facts and data, aided by intuition and experience. As you work through this tool, refer to learning and conclusions from prior tools. Or, return to those tools to refresh the work and your thinking. In particular, consider the **Gap Analysis Tool**, a critical input for setting priorities.

A word about strategy. In business, strategy occurs on three levels: Enterprise, Operational and Tactical. If chess is the ultimate strategy game, executing strategy is like playing chess on three levels simultaneously. Successful strategy execution relies on everyone in the organization knowing the objectives and how each contributes to the whole. Establishing a common understanding of the three levels of strategy helps. We've included our view and things to consider in the table **Clarify Your Terms**.

Set priorities to close gaps, capture opportunities, and reach your destination.

Strategic Planning

STEP 1	STEP 2	STEP 3
Brainstorm Potential Focus Areas	**Select 3-5 Strategic Priorities**	**Create Strategic Plan**

KEY ACTIONS (Step 1)

- Brainstorm potential focus areas
  - Refer to opportunities list, gap analysis, and shared understanding of markets, competitors, and customers
- Confirm all are at the Enterprise level
  - Meaningful to your vision
  - Serve organization-wide objective
- Enhance clarity and assure shared understanding of potential, high-level priorities

KEY ACTIONS (Step 2)

- Consider attractiveness and fit of each priority
- Assess relative level of effort, importance for the vision, and strategic impact of each priority
  - Draw on Decision Tools
- Choose top 3-5 priorities
  - Areas on which you will focus
  - These are the foundation of your strategy
- Articulate and share enterprise level strategic priorities

KEY ACTIONS (Step 3)

- Create high-level action plan and timeline for enterprise priorities
  - Assign accountabilities for executing critical pieces of plan
- Establish metrics, baseline, milestones for enterprise plan
- Operationalize the enterprise plan
  - Cascade priorities and metrics
  - Detail action plans to advance strategic priorities for each functional and operational area
- Set protocol to monitor progress
  - Regular, ongoing review
  - Review prompted by a warning flag, signaling change in conditions

The **Strategic Planning Roadmap** focuses on how to set priorities that close the gaps, capture opportunities, and guide you in achieving the vision. It's written for the Enterprise level, yet can be adapted for use at the Operational level. Set the Enterprise level first. From there, each operational leader uses a similar, subsequent process to describe how their function or team contributes to the company strategy. In effect, each operational unit creates its own enterprise strategy that must fit within the context of the company's priorities and Enterprise-level strategy. For all, the tactics should support the overall plan and help to achieve the vision. Use both the Enterprise and Operational plans to make decisions about which tactics you really need—and adapt these as conditions change.

The key outcome of strategic planning is the handful of priorities on which you'll focus to achieve your vision. The **Prioritization Aid** suggests a path to set priorities. In the **Examples**, you'll see alternative ways to present and track actions over time.

Yet, a strategic plan is not a blueprint with step-by-step instructions. In keeping with our journey metaphor, you can't simply set a GPS for your strategy and forget it. Strategy execution is active and fluid; it's made up of decisions and actions that address obstacles or opportunities *as they arise*. Done well, strategic planning makes it easier to execute strategy and to actively manage the balance between strategy and operations.

TABLE

Clarify Your Terms

	Enterprise	Operational	Tactical
	30,000-foot view	*15,000-foot view*	*Ground level view*
Answers the questions	How will we **focus** to take the **entire company** forward?	How does our **unit's expertise** contribute to the Enterprise?	How do we get this done **together**?
Requires these behaviors	Senior leaders think for the benefit of the organization. Do not rest solely in their own domains	Operational leaders continually reflect up to address Enterprise implications; coordinate tactical (down)	Managers at all levels mobilize everyone in the organization
Includes these elements	• **Highest level** perspective starting with mission, vision, values • **Holistic**, looking across lines of business, functions, and units, bringing together the parts into a cohesive whole • **Connected**, requiring collaboration and shared objectives	• **Broad**, focusing on how the expertise of each area or function contributes to the Enterprise • **Deep**, drilling down into various lines of business of business and functions • **Interdependent**, considering relationships across and within organizational boundaries and relationships	• **Detailed implementation** of actions on the ground • **Task-oriented**, focusing on what each person or area does on a regular basis to implement a priority • **Individual contributions**, focusing on what individuals or small groups do to accomplish priorities

 AID

Prioritization

Use a structured approach to consider and select your priorities.

Brainstorm a list of potential strategic focus areas	Consider	Use
Identify capabilities and resources most important to achieve your vision • Ensure they are at enterprise or company level • Balance the specific (we all understand what to do) with broad (we can adapt as conditions change and we learn along the journey) • Avoid jargon; keep it simple and succinct	• Which focus areas are most strategic? • Which have the greatest likelihood for success? • Which are the easiest or require less effort? • What will it take to pursue these priorities? • What will it take to pursue t areas that are both strategic and likely to succeed, but also hard to do? • What does this analysis tell us about the urgency or order of pursuing these opportunities? • What is the opportunity cost of pursuing these versus something else? • Can we do these? Do we *want* to?	• Decision tools to ease the process and focus on quality, fact-based discussion

Reshape and select strategic priorities to gain clarity and agreement.

Strategic Planning

Three-year plan to reach the vision.

Area/Department	Action	Leaders	Q1 2020	Q2 2020	Q3 2020	Q4 2020	Q1 2021	Q2 2021	--	Q4 2022
1. Finance		Mrs. X								
	New ERP system				█	█	█	█	█	
	Outsource payroll				█	█	█	█	█	█
	Reduce closing cycle to Day + 5									█
2. Commercial		Mr. Y								
	Develop Commercial Strategy			█						
	Eliminate Industrial customer segment				█	█				
	Move into international markets: Asia									█
3. Human Resources		Miss Z								
	Etc…				█					

Destination: VISION

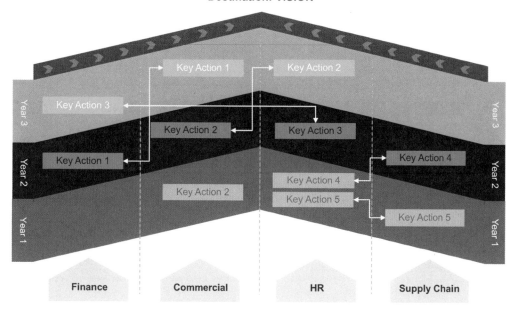

Interdependencies between departments

Strategic Planning

EXAMPLE

Strategic Plan

Craft a detailed action list and timeline for each priority. Then sort by year to test and finalize your strategic plan for the entire enterprise.

Execution Planning: Enterprise Level

Strategic Priority: Build core competence in customer and business intelligence (to attract and serve) a broader universe of prospective customers

Sponsors: Mary Shelley   **Update:**

Key Action / Initiative	Responsible Area / Person	2015	2016				2017				2018				2019				Status
		Q4	Q1	Q2	Q3	Q4	Q1	Q2	Q3	Q4	Q1	Q2	Q3	Q4	Q1	Q2	Q3	Q4	

Key Milestones or Performance Metrics	Current Level	Target	By When

Looking at all priorities and actions, consider to what extent:
- Is the timeline reasonable?
- Is the work distributed well?
- Are these actions interdependent?

Strategic plans describe your focus areas and critical actions.

Enterprise level strategic priorities guide you for the next few years.

- They should not be easily achieved or changed

They must be both sufficiently specific *and* flexible to allow you to make hard decisions about what you should or should not do.

- We must be able to interpret them at operational and functional levels

Enterprise level strategy spans the entire organization, creating priorities that are holistic and likely interdependent.

- Manage interdependencies well to execute strategy effectively
- Choose metrics that help you understand how well the parts work together

Remember to assign accountability for executing each strategic priority.

- Look across specific areas to know who's leading what, as they manage their own contributions to achieving the vision

Strategic plans are not the same as project plans.

- They are paths to reach critical milestones, an approximate timeline, and accountability
- They show how various parts must come together to make it work
- They do <u>not</u> detail every step required to reach the destination

Strategic Planning

Strategic Dashboard

Many of you may be familiar with Key Performance Indicators—or KPIs—as well as other reports that help you track progress or compare planned versus actual activities and results. Think about a monthly report of budget vs. actual results, for example. Typically, those are terrific tools for tracking operating progress and near-term fluctuations.

 ROADMAP

Four steps to develop a Strategic Dashboard.

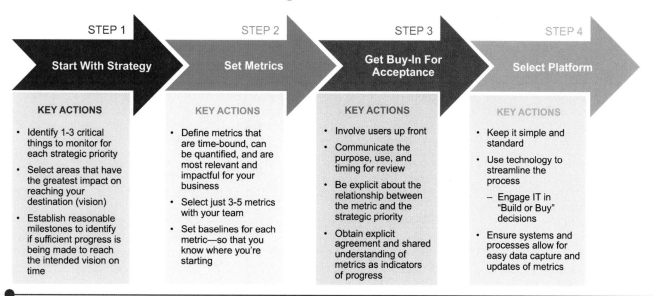

STEP 1	STEP 2	STEP 3	STEP 4
Start With Strategy	**Set Metrics**	**Get Buy-In For Acceptance**	**Select Platform**
KEY ACTIONS	**KEY ACTIONS**	**KEY ACTIONS**	**KEY ACTIONS**
• Identify 1-3 critical things to monitor for each strategic priority • Select areas that have the greatest impact on reaching your destination (vision) • Establish reasonable milestones to identify if sufficient progress is being made to reach the intended vision on time	• Define metrics that are time-bound, can be quantified, and are most relevant and impactful for your business • Select just 3-5 metrics with your team • Set baselines for each metric—so that you know where you're starting	• Involve users up front • Communicate the purpose, use, and timing for review • Be explicit about the relationship between the metric and the strategic priority • Obtain explicit agreement and shared understanding of metrics as indicators of progress	• Keep it simple and standard • Use technology to streamline the process – Engage IT in "Build or Buy" decisions • Ensure systems and processes allow for easy data capture and updates of metrics

Ideally, they also include both leading and lagging indicators so that you obtain a snapshot of where you are in any given moment. We call those Scorecards. They help you keep the lights on (and are super important as you manage your journey, which we'll discuss in more detail in Section 3).

A **Strategic Dashboard** is something different altogether. In our experience, the use of a strategic dashboard is much less common than it should be.

As its name suggests, a strategic dashboard helps you keep your eye on the destination—much as a car's dashboard provides specific metrics to guide progress when you travel. The odometer tracks distance covered. The speedometer monitors your rate of travel, and fuel, temperature, and fluid gauges measure your fitness to continue the journey. Similarly, a strategic dashboard monitors the ongoing fitness of the organization to reach its vision. It highlights the critical few things needed to close the gap between where you are and where you want to be, and by when.

> **Unlike KPIs or other scorecards, a strategic dashboard promotes a forward-looking perspective that goes beyond the activities required to manage day-to-day realities.**

Unlike KPIs or other scorecards, a strategic dashboard promotes a forward-looking perspective that goes beyond the activities required to manage day-to-day realities. It focuses attention on the longer-term strategic priorities. And, because these priorities are often interdependent, it's particularly useful to highlight and monitor them in one place. It also helps bring strategy to life by tying the high-level priorities to measurable indicators of progress that can be tracked over set time frames.

We've summarized the distinction between **Strategic Dashboard** and **Scorecard** in the following table.

Clarify Your Terms

Strategic Dashboard	Scorecard
Serves this purpose	A **Strategic Dashboard** keeps your eye on the destination (vision)	A **Scorecard** helps you keep the lights on
Highlights these markers	• Focuses on **longer-term milestones** that describe success in achieving the vision • Provides a quick overview of progress on the (often interdependent) **strategic priorities** • Monitors the ***ongoing* fitness** of the organization to reach its destination • Highlights the **critical few** things you need to stay the course and head in the right direction	• Measures and compares **operating performance** against **near-term** projections and goals • Evaluates success and failure of your efforts, based on **key performance indicators.** • Includes **leading and lagging** indicators to deal with challenges, or capture opportunities *as they arise* • Provides a snapshot of where you are in any given **moment**
Resembles this	 *A car's dashboard is strategic, with specific metrics to gauge progress toward the destination (odometer, speed) and your fitness to continue (fuel, temperature)*	 *Tire pressure and check engine lights are operating metrics; they alert you to very specific, near-term issues you must address immediately to keep moving*

In many ways, the **Roadmap** to develop a strategic dashboard is relatively simple. The dashboard should be a reflection of what you and your executive team have discussed and agreed in terms of where you'll focus and what success looks like. That guides your choice of metrics, and—to the extent you've involved the right people in developing your strategy—fosters a shared understanding of the baseline, what it will take to achieve the vision, and by when. As you plan your journey, you'll set your current position and targets at agreed times (e.g., 6 months, 2 years). Obtaining buy-in for acceptance of these targets at the outset makes it easier and more meaningful later to compare actual progress versus your target, and to reveal gaps in capabilities and resources.

Above all, keep it simple—both to read and to use. If it's too hard to update or interpret, it won't be used. The **Examples** of strategic dashboards that we've provided illustrate two very simple, meaningful dashboards used by our clients.

Done well, the strategic dashboard is a tool to build strategic agility among your executive team and your board. Use it to identify specific insights, frame decisions, and take specific actions. The executive team and board play different roles in helping you to execute strategy well. Consequently, as you share the dashboard, first consider what decisions you need from each audience (executive team and board). That can guide your conversation and ensure each group contributes appropriately to managing strategy. Always articulate the business impact of your progress (or lack thereof), and how it relates to each audience's role and the decisions you expect from them. Rather than arguing about the data, generate discussion about the challenges and opportunities, then identify or share specific actions or responses to adapt your strategy. You may need new behaviors or competencies, or additional resources. There may be critical derailers you must mitigate or eliminate entirely. Ongoing course evaluation and correction are among the most important things you can do to keep strategy on track.

Large, Complex Organization

The strategic dashboard measures fiscal stability, visitor experience, environmental impact, and operational efficiency.

Strategic Dashboard

Operating Efficiency Op Margin/Customer	**Funding Source** % Non-gate Revenue	**Development Efficiency** Funds as % Cost of Fundraising
Capitalization As % Current (Opex+CapEx+Debt Service)	**# Organizational Agility** Collective ease of/ability to get things done Employee satisfaction rating	**Environmental Impact** # Conservation Actions Avg Participation Rate
# Relationships # Encounters/Customer	**Customer ROI** % overall, by customer type	**Experience Effectiveness** % Excellent Overall Satisfaction Word of Month

Source: Strategy for Real. Used with permission.

Strategic Dashboard

EXAMPLE

Strategic Dashboard

Small or Simple Organization

This smaller, less complex organization focuses on sustained revenue.

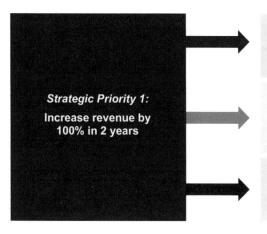

Strategic Priority 1:

Increase revenue by 100% in 2 years

Action 1: Develop 2-3 key clients by 2021.

- Cultivate new relationships with 2 multi-unit clients annually
- Establish multi-year engagements or services

Action 2: Increase referrals.

- Deliver excellent results for clients, resulting in 1-2 specific referrals
- Increase visibility as 'expert' via speaking (2 in 2020, 4 in 2021), social media, and blog (bi-monthly)

Action 3: Penetrate 1 new market in 2020.

- Establish 2 new partnerships in 2019 to serve public sector beginning in 2020
- Develop 1 new service

Source: Strategy for Real. Used with permission.

Embed strategic review into ongoing management processes

Review Cycle

Monthly Management Meeting

Strategic Priority: _____

Action Step: _____

Quarterly Review

Strategic Priority: _____

Action Step: _____

Budget or Operating Review

Strategic Priority: _____

Action Step: _____

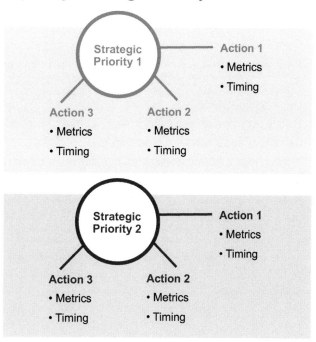

Source: Strategy for Real. Used with permission.

Strategic Dashboard

Strategic Dashboard

How to create a meaningful strategic dashboard:

Do:

- Keep it simple
- Make it visually appealing and easy to use/maintain
- Match your dashboard to your vision, values, and strategic priorities
- Present a high-level perspective (full business, enterprise-level, end-to-end process)
- Use aggregated rather than detailed data: less is more
- Include both hard and soft metrics (e.g., ROI, margins, ratios, survey data, etc.)
- Use graphs and charts to highlight trends
- Identify specific measurement intervals over time (past and current quarter, year, etc.)
- Choose metrics and a format to promote actionable insights
- Know the audience and their role; tailor the dashboard to the decisions each will make

Don't:

- Merge your strategic, operational, and tactical dashboards; each serves a different purpose
- Expect to make complex decisions based on these metric; instead, raise questions and identify opportunities for further analysis
- Lose sight of the destination—and the outcome (behaviors, results, etc.) you want to achieve

Capital Investment Visibility

Planning and monitoring your capital expenditure well can create additional value for your business. That's why we created a tool to enhance the visibility of your capital expenditure (CapEx) program, not just when the initial capital investment decisions are taken, but also as expenditures are made and value is created. While the monitoring part occurs as you manage your journey (Section 3), planning CapEx is very much a strategic process. Using the same structured framework for CapEx—as we've suggested in our **Capital Investment Visibility Tool**—makes it easier to ensure the expenditures remain linked to strategy over time. In that way, it's another tool which furthers the balance between strategy and operations.

Capital expenditures are often part of a project, program, or change in equipment or facilities. At the enterprise level, CapEx is reflected as an aggregated number, offering little insight into how well money has been allocated. Further, capital expenditures are depreciated or amortized over time—which dilutes the impact of your spending on your results in any given time period. Many CEOs don't think of CapEx in the same way as they do other financial or operating metrics. Yet, a mismanaged CapEx plan can smother growth. That's why CEOs benefit when they make their capital investment visible and actively monitor it.

Capital expenditure planning is the process by which an organization allocates capital to support both growth and on-going business needs. Importantly, you should be allocating resources based on the strategic priorities you've identified. That includes not only the new capital you'll spend, but also, how much capital (and resources) you'll allocate to ongoing business needs. CapEx monitoring is a separate and distinct process that helps to effectively manage the portfolio of selected projects or programs.

 ROADMAP

An iterative process with active monitoring and adjustments.

Capital Investment Visibility

STEP 1	STEP 2	STEP 3	STEP 4
CapEx Planning	**Selection Process**	**Monitoring**	**Portfolio Optimization**

KEY ACTIONS

- Set overall CapEx budget in alignment with strategic and operational needs (can be iterative)
- Split CapEx into relevant buckets (growth, maintenance, compliance)
- Use bottom-up approach to establish list of potential projects

KEY ACTIONS

- Form a CapEx committee and clarify its roles
- Set project selection criteria and approval matrix
- Agree on framework for taking funding decisions

KEY ACTIONS

- Identify metrics for individual projects and overall (e.g., NPV, payback, IRR, hurdle rates, etc.)
- Establish reporting timeline and standard format
- Assign reporting accountability

KEY ACTIONS

- Regularly update project business cases
  - Benchmark across the organization and competitors to identify areas of improvement
  - Perform post-mortem analysis to identify lessons learned
- Rebalance spend as conditions shift

The need for ongoing planning, evaluation, reassessment, and adjustment is reflected in our **Capital Investment Visibility Roadmap**. This requires an iterative process with active monitoring and adjustment. In our experience, leadership teams typically embrace an established process to plan capital expenditures. Selecting and monitoring CapEx—the steps that really help to make capital investment visible—are often less-disciplined or structured. Our **Aids** and **Examples** focus on those steps.

Using the same structured framework to both plan and monitor your CapEx helps you to think holistically and to see the entire portfolio in the same format. That also streamlines decisions. Ideally, you want to focus on the overall portfolio value rather than individual projects or programs, particularly since each will have a different timeline or maturity that impacts its value creation potential. Consider creating or using a corporate level steering committee to choose capital investments that benefit the whole company. Treat capital expenditure project management as a professional function; success requires competence in *both* finance and project management.

 AID

CapEx Project Selection: Step 1

For each selection category, list common criteria to evaluate your CapEx projects.

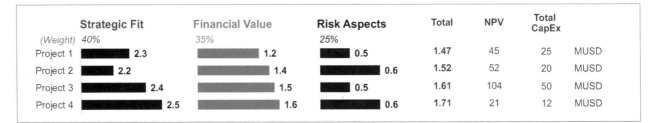

	Strategic Fit 40%	Financial Value 35%	Risk Aspects 25%	Total	NPV	Total CapEx	
Project 1	2.3	1.2	0.5	1.47	45	25	MUSD
Project 2	2.2	1.4	0.6	1.52	52	20	MUSD
Project 3	2.4	1.5	0.5	1.61	104	50	MUSD
Project 4	2.5	1.6	0.6	1.71	21	12	MUSD

Strategic Fit

- Impact on production capacity, upgrade plan
- Impact on partnerships, customers, reputation, brand
- Further CapEx required to achieve desired state
- Competitive positioning

Financial Value

- Ability to self-finance
- Investment structure (control / JV / minority holding)
- Availability of alternative options, ability to postpone
- Financial risk

Risk Aspects

- Technical risk
- Project implementation risks
- Third party risks (partners, suppliers)
- Organizational risks
- Strength of mitigation plan

Evaluation criteria for each category: Agree on criteria that makes sense for your business.

Capital Investment Visibility

 AID

CapEx Project Selection: Step 2

For each project, qualify and quantify your evaluation.

Project A: Invest US$25M (including US$1M capitalized interest)

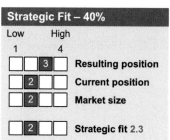

Strategic Fit – 40%		
Low 1	High 4	
3		Resulting position
2		Current position
2		Market size
2		Strategic fit 2.3

- Financially attractive market with limited or low industry risk level
- Rare new market entrants

Financial Value – 35%		
Low 1	High 4	
1		IRR
1		Hurdle Rate
2		NPV
1		Financial Value 1.2

- Attractive financial valuation
- Multiple financing options available
- Investment cost-estimate based on firm offers

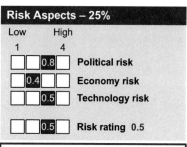

Risk Aspects – 25%		
Low 1	High 4	
0.8		Political risk
0.4		Economy risk
0.5		Technology risk
0.5		Risk rating 0.5

- New technology still in pre-production phase
- New geography for us with upcoming elections
- One of the fastest growing economies

Step 3

Select projects based on ranking outcome

Overall rating : 1.47

Capital Investment Visibility

AID

Stoplight CapEx Scorecard

Create Stoplight CapEx Scorecard to monitor status of projects and overall program—showing snapshot and trends.

Capital Expenditure Monitoring Dashboard

Review Date: Jan-18

Monitored Topics

Projects list

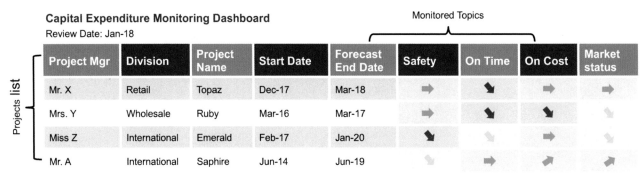

Project Mgr	Division	Project Name	Start Date	Forecast End Date	Safety	On Time	On Cost	Market status
Mr. X	Retail	Topaz	Dec-17	Mar-18	→	↘	→	→
Mrs. Y	Wholesale	Ruby	Mar-16	Mar-17	→	↘	↘	↘
Miss Z	International	Emerald	Feb-17	Jan-20	↘		→	↘
Mr. A	International	Saphire	Jun-14	Jun-19		→	↗	↗

Legend

Safety	On Time	On Cost	Market status
0 incident	On time	Forecast = budget	
1-5 incidents	Less than 3 months late	Forecast = budget + 20%	
6+ incidents	More than 3 months late	Forecast > budget + 20%	

- *Stoplight colors (red, yellow, green) illustrate status quickly.*

- *Arrow indicators suggest trends (up ↗ , down ↘ , steady-on ➡) versus prior time period.*

 AID

Monitoring CapEx Checklist

☐ **Centralize overall CapEx program oversight to gain visibility into capital spending across the organization**

☐ **Encourage reuse of equipment, tools, etc., by creating a link between Capital Expenditure and Asset Management staff or departments.**

☐ **Incorporate three into your decision and monitoring tools:**
    ☐ A methodology that quantifies value and risk to effectively prioritize projects
    ☐ Fiscal aspects of the project and broader implications across your portfolio
    ☐ Operational metrics to gauge progress or highlight needed adjustments

☐ **Review specifically and regularly:**
    ☐ The details of the money spent and actual versus desired returns from investments
    ☐ The speed at which the project is implemented
    ☐ Current market conditions and strategic fit; different conditions may alter fit

Capital Investment Visibility

EXAMPLE

Capital Investment Visibility

Technology CapEx Program

Map estimated capital expenditure over multiple years to gain better visibility.

Three-year IT CapEx Plan				
2020 Projects	**Description/Comments**	**Geography**	**Product Line**	**Amount**
Access control system		Europe	Retail	$55K
Life cycle management	Replace 1/3 of PCs	All	All	$60K
Company website upgrade	More interactive Portal	All	All	$20K
Address Cyber security risk	Increase systems ability	Global	All	$150K
Total				$285K
2021 Projects	**Description/Comments**	**Geography**	**Product Line**	**Amount**
ERP implementation	Replace Finance-Procurement	N. America	All	$350K
Customer Portal	Implement			
E-Procurement platform	New tool integrated into ERP	Global	All	$120K
Life Cycle Management	Replace 1/3 of PCs	All	All	$60K
Total				$530K
2022 Projects	**Description/Comments**	**Geography**	**Product Line**	**Amount**
Life Cycle Management	Replace 1/3 of PCs	All	All	$60K
Move to Data Center	Move internal servers to cloud based solution	All	All	$80K
Total				$140K

ACCELERATION TIPS

Take the emotion out of the decision making and planning process.
- Use a multidisciplinary, transparent approach to eliminate bias as much as possible
- Consider electronic workflow for approval facilitation and as a data source
- Establish regular status reports from the start, including standard formats to allow for better portfolio comparison
- Communicate frequently to the right people

Evaluate value generated from your portfolio.
- Reset CapEx amounts as time goes on and project dynamics change
- Re-run business cases multiple times throughout the life cycle
- Benchmark against your competitors, as well as across your own projects

Increase project return accountability:
- Establish an incentive system to reward the best project teams
- Allocate funding down to direct ownership level

Capital Investment Visibility

Risk Assessment

No strategy or plan is complete without establishing a solid understanding of risk.

By definition, uncertainty abounds in strategic planning. If we knew all the answers, had perfect information, and nothing ever changed, we'd probably make the right business calls and achieve our vision every time. Sad truth: that Pollyanna world simply doesn't exist. In fact, that inherent uncertainty and ambiguity in our strategic thinking and planning breeds risk. As CEO, you guide your team to identify and assess the risks regularly. Together, you take decisions and incorporate the necessary actions into your strategic plan to mitigate those risks (See **Effective Decisions Tool**).

Risks come in many shapes and forms, and from many different directions—such as the global COVID-19 pandemic in 2020. We've found it helpful to classify the risks, based on simple, agreed categories that help you to make sense of them. Those categories create an instant framework founded on a common language about the types of risks you may face. Identifying specific vulnerabilities and the sources of risk, rather than just the risk itself, also helps you to avoid surprises and possibly to anticipate potential new risks that may emerge along the way.

Like strategy, risks occur on multiple levels. Some risks or hazards have potential impacts across the entire enterprise; others may be more important for specific units or departments. Our **Risk Assessment Roadmap** outlines three steps to help you understand and focus on the potential risks that could have the greatest impact on your ability to achieve your vision. Incorporate these actively into your ongoing strategic review. For example, as you scan your **External Landscape** to monitor what's changed or emerging, identify the implications for the potential risks you've identified and adapt your mitigation strategies accordingly.

Manage exposure to/impact of potential risks in executing your strategy.

Risk Assessment

| STEP 1 | STEP 2 | STEP 3 |

Assess Potential Risks | **Identify Critical Risks** | **Develop Risk Management Strategy**

KEY ACTIONS
- Brainstorm risk factors that have the potential to impede progress toward the vision
- Assess specific vulnerabilities
- Identify potential impacts

KEY ACTIONS
- Analyze impacts
- Characterize likelihood of occurrence
- Define the resources needed to mitigate or eliminate
- Select the risks with the greatest potential to disrupt strategy

KEY ACTIONS
- Identify actions to mitigate or eliminate risks
- Make contingency plans
- Update risk controls and embed in regular processes
- Monitor risks and readiness

Risks also impact stakeholder groups in different ways. Stakeholders can be both a help and a hindrance when you are addressing risks. Map stakeholder influence and satisfaction so that you understand in what ways your stakeholders might help you to mitigate risk—or to identify areas of weakness in those relationships. Often a crisis originates from the stakeholder group with the least satisfaction with your organization. Identify the actions you can take to leverage or mitigate them, ideally before the crisis happens.

By now, it's probably clear that risk assessment can be rather challenging. No single methodology works for all organizations and situations. Fortunately, many tools are available, ranging from very simple to complex. We've included **Aids** and **Examples** of risk assessments for different levels of the organization and a stakeholder map to give you a sense of what others have done to assess, monitor, and manage their risks. Choose the practices and tools that work best for your organization. Above all, set time and assign accountability to monitor risks regularly.

AID

Checklist to Improve Risk Exposure Management

1. Determine risk sources and categories

☐ Identify hazards, risk sources, and risk factors with potential to cause harms to your business
☐ Scan externally and internally for risk sources
☐ Categorize the types of hazards (e.g., human, operating, financial, community, reputation, etc.)
☐ Document risks in your Risk Register

2. Assess vulnerabilities

☐ List all assets to identify which may be at risk
☐ Assess vulnerabilities—what makes an asset more or less susceptible to damage from a hazard
☐ Determine each asset's vulnerability relative priority

3. Analyze impacts

☐ Run "what if" scenarios to identify what could happen and to whom if the hazard/condition was to occur
☐ Qualify and, if possible, quantify the risk level for each hazard
☐ Focus on areas and activities that are critical to your success

4. Establish risk management strategy

☐ Determine appropriate ways to eliminate the hazard, manage the risk, or limit its impact
☐ Make contingency plans for residual risk (e.g., disaster recovery, succession, or emergency plans)
☐ Establish an organizational policy for planning and performing the risk management process

5. Review risk controls

☐ Include risk control reviews in your regular processes (e.g., Internal Audit, Internal Control Plans)
☐ Test your controls to regulate your assumptions
☐ Provide adequate resources for performing the risk management process

Risk Assessment

AID

Identifying Hazards & Risk Factors

Ask questions to identify hazards and risk factors.

- What is most likely to derail you?
- What will throw off your projections?
- What would impede access to resources?
- What would make it significantly harder to meet stakeholder expectations (including delivering products or services)?
- What is most likely to cause your customers to lose faith in your organization, products or services?
- Where are hazards most likely to come from?
  - Weather, competition, human error, process, regulation, access to capital, inflation, political unrest, terrorism, biological, etc.

Stakeholder Influence Map

Stakeholder	Organization	Influence (positive, negative, neutral)	Geographic Influence (local, national, regional, global)	Influence Level (very low, low, average, high)	Stakeholder Satisfaction (very low, low, average, high)	Action
Media	TV Channel 5	Negative	Local	High	Low	Develop better relationships
Environment	EPA	Negative	National	High	Low	Be proactive in monitoring their mood
Employees	Retirees	Positive	Local	Low	High	Incorporate them into outreach campaigns as goodwill ambassadors
Customers	ABC Co (our largest & most prominent customer)	Positive	Regional	Average	Average	Monitor: e.g., not happy with last price increase

Risk Assessment

Enterprise-wide Risk Assessment

Risk Assessment

Threat/Risk Category	Vulnerability	Asset	Impact	Risk Level	Response
Natural disaster – e.g., hurricane, flood, earthquake	No raised floor in computer room	Servers	Unavailability of certain services (email, website, ERP, etc.)	High ($100K)	Install raised floor in Computer room
	Loss of communications	Employees, Customers, Stakeholders	Inability to reach people and find out their status	Medium	Update contact list and outreach communication tree
	Production disruption	Manufacturing facility	Inability to serve customers	High ($250K)	Keep six-week safety stock during hurricane season
Hazardous material leak in manufacturing facility	Containment walls not high enough	Manufacturing facility – waste area	Community, damage to company image, loss of operating license	High ($5M)	Reinforce walls and revisit emergency plan (including communication plan)
Road Safety	Sales representatives on the road many hours everyday	Salespeople	Bodily injury in case of accident; diminished capacity	Medium	Revisit safety policy to include mandatory wear of seatbelts, speed limits; no phone usage while driving

Others...

Departmental-Level Risk Assessment

HR Challenges	Risk Level	Response
High percentage of key employees may retire within next 3 years	High	Launch a recruitment program for High Potential employees and revisit succession plan
No reliable data on HR costs	Medium	Add a comptroller to the HR team
Administrative burden passed on the Business partners due to insufficient HR resources and tools	Low	Isolate these processes, identify costs vs. value, take a process improvement approach and push back hard
Limited HR talent can meet the company's new challenges	Medium	Perform formal assessment of HR talent pool. Develop the top talents, replace the mediocre ones, Develop a strong HR onboarding program.
Recruiting pressures are back due to company growth phase	High	Externalize the recruiting process
Others...		

Risk Assessment

AID

Deep-Dive Risk Assessment: Specific Risk Category

Cyber Security Risk: Events may occur which will impact the company's ability to protect its systems, networks, and programs from digital attacks that impact sensitive information, user integrity, or interrupt normal business processes.

Consider the questions in each category. Use your answers to evaluate the risk in terms of its impact and likelihood, and your ability to mitigate. 1 – Insignificant 2 – Minor 3 – Moderate 4 – Significant 5 – Material	Significance of Impact	Likelihood of Occurrence	Effectiveness of Ability to Mitigate Occurrence or Impact	Comments (Clarify response to enhance understanding of exposure)
1. Security Policy Risk • Is Security Policy approved by Management? • Is it communicated to employees and stakeholders? • Is it revised every 12 months? • Do you have a Security Policy Training?				
2. Organizational Security Risk • Do you perform ongoing security monitoring? • Do you perform an IT security risk assessment on third parties that have access to your systems and data?				
3. Operational Security Risk • Do you have a documented change management policy? • Do you have an anti-virus/malware policy or program? • Are encrypted data backups performed? • Are firewalls in use and properly configured for both internal and external connections? • Do you have a password policy that enforces the use of unique passwords, complexity, expiration, reuse, etc.? • Do you log data for incident response and forensic investigation? Are the logs reviewed on a regular basis?				

Cyber Security Risk: Events may occur which will impact the company's ability to protect its systems, networks, and programs from digital attacks that impact sensitive information, user integrity, or interrupt normal business processes.

1 – Insignificant 2 – Minor 3 – Moderate
4 – Significant 5 – Material

	Significance of Impact	Likelihood of Occurrence	Effectiveness of Ability to Mitigate Occurrence or Impact	Comments (Clarify response to enhance understanding of exposure)
4. Access Control Risk • Is there a documented access control policy? • Are unique user IDs used for access? • Is single-sign-on (SSO) / shared authentication implemented and available? • Is there a password policy ? • Is there a remote access?				
5. Mobile Device/Use Risk • Do you have a documented policy for mobile device use? • Does the security policy include a requirement for mobile device management and mobile application management (MDM and MAM)?				
6. Application Development Risk • If application development is performed, does your development team adhere to a formal application security methods?				

Note: *If you use cloud services, consider adding a category to assess the risks for your organization that are tailored to the specific agreement with and services of your cloud provider*

ACCELERATION TIPS

Include qualitative and quantitative aspects in your risk analysis.
- **Quantitative** risk analysis assigns numeric monetary values to each different risk assessment component, and to the level of potential losses
- **Qualitative** risk analysis is scenario-based with different threat-vulnerability scenarios, "what if" type of questions

Make risk assessment a regular part of the organization's internal processes (quality assurance, security, project management, etc.).
- Compliance risk assessment is critical for highly regulated industries (e.g., banking, cement, energy, agriculture) and publicly traded companies

Keep the human impact in mind when identifying risks.
- Human impact also directly affects business—no matter what business you are in

The intangible is as important as the tangible.
- Consider the impact an incident could have on relationships with customers, the surrounding community, and other stakeholders.

Section 3: Manage Your Journey

When traveling, you do not simply 'set and forget' your navigation system.

Every member of your group has a role in monitoring progress and managing the journey; each person provides critical information and insight. Together, you listen to the updates, process new information, and decide what to do next. All that data helps you to discern when to regroup or make adjustments so that you reach the destination most effectively and efficiently.

The same is true in business. Once the strategy is set and teams are empowered to move forward, leaders must continue to monitor progress and manage breakdowns. Of course, that sounds obvious; yet, that's often the most challenging part of achieving the vision. And, the journey rarely goes as planned. Just as drivers must remain constantly alert so that they do not lose control of the car, so too must the CEO and senior leaders continue to monitor the dashboard and continuously link daily activities and operating decisions to strategic priorities.

It's easy to get lost in the activities of your daily work. As you move forward, take time to ask questions and rethink conventional wisdom. We've included a few questions to get you started.

Questions to Consider:

- What do our operating metrics tell us about our performance over time? Are the trends positive or negative?
- Will the business metrics we've chosen allow us to anticipate issues?
- Is everyone clear about the expectations for their role and contribution to success?
- Are the organization and each team equipped to meet the next milestone or challenge? Do we have the right capabilities?
- To what extent is our approach to performance management meaningful in developing our people and meeting our business objectives?
- How will we hold people accountable?
- How well do we know our Board? How well do we work together?
- What will we do when a crisis strikes? How prepared do we feel?

How To Use The Tools To Manage The Journey:

Tools in this section enhance the ability of the organization to actually deliver against the objectives set by senior leaders. Using the **Operational Execution Tool**, create an **Operational Scorecard** that complements your **Strategic Dashboard** and holds people accountable. The scorecard creates one of the most visible links between strategy and operations. It describes the specific operating actions required for each strategic priority, plus specific metrics to gauge progress. Framing operational activities in the context of your strategic priorities helps to ensure that you are both delivering on current promises and expectations, and building toward the future.

A big piece of closing the gap between where you are and where you want to go involves capabilities—both organizational and individual. Ideally, you assessed both of these before defining your plan (See **Gap Analysis** and **Strategic Planning Tools**). Your environment is not static. Review capabilities at least annually, to ensure your organization and your people are equipped to shift direction quickly and effectively. Use the **Organizational Capabilities Tool** to assess the readiness of the organization as a whole. The **Performance Management Tool** considers current performance and helps you to create a plan to improve or expand capabilities for individuals.

Finally, we include tools to deal with crises as they occur (**Crisis Management**), and one to leverage your Board of Directors or Advisors (**Strong Board Relations**). Use the **Crisis Management Tool** to be ready to navigate a crisis so that you may mitigate its broader impact and get back on track more quickly. Managed well, your Board can be a powerful ally, in any situation.

> Framing operational activities in the context of your strategic priorities helps to ensure that you are both delivering on current promises and expectations, and building toward the future.

During this phase, you are actively measuring the alignment and balance between strategy and operations. Successful leaders make this a routine part of running their businesses.

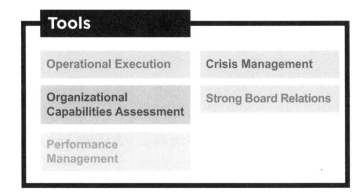

Tools

Operational Execution	Crisis Management
Organizational Capabilities Assessment	Strong Board Relations
Performance Management	

Dive into the Tools:

Operational Execution

"It's all about execution."

No doubt you've heard that statement repeatedly. And it's valid. A strategy that you cannot (or do not) execute is worthless to your company. **Operational Execution** links the high-level strategic priorities you created for the Enterprise to the more specific things you'll do to achieve your vision. Operational excellence is about doing this very, very well. It's a delicate balance of efficiency and effectiveness that results in a highly productive, skilled workforce that is committed equally to maintaining daily operations and doing their level best to drive strategy forward.

CEOs set the foundation for success. They align people and assure the structures and systems are established and working well to achieve the objectives. Yet inevitably, there will be breakdowns; amid an ever-changing environment, not all will go as planned. The best you can (and should!) do is to monitor performance, anticipate shifts, and manage the breakdowns effectively. That helps you to uncover trends—good and bad—and adapt to emerging opportunities or challenges as they arise.

Monitoring trends in business performance is much easier using a common format and specific intervals at which to check your company's "gauges." In Section 2, we shared a **Strategic Dashboard** and talked about the difference between a scorecard and a dashboard in the table on page 109. We've included an operational scorecard example that measures the ongoing health of the business over time. That's a key piece of operational execution. It aligns and focuses all operating and functional units around one standard for success, and creates a habit of measuring and monitoring progress.

ROADMAP

Operational execution includes four steps in a nearly continuous loop to manage the journey.

1. Cascade the Strategic Priorities

- Set priorities for operating or functional areas based on company priorities
- Articulate how each area contributes to overall strategy
- Identify those priorities most relevant to your areas:
  - Greatest impact on reaching the destination
  - Most needed to maintain the business

2. Detail the Action Plans

- Expand company route plan
- Detail the actions and contributions from your team
  - Include specific financial impacts
- Determine who does what, by when

3. Measure & Monitor

- Identify your key performance indicators to monitor health and show progress
- Set baselines and timeline for measurement
- Create a simple format for reporting
  - Use company-wide tools as available

4. Create Accountability

- Define consequences & rewards
- Communicate results
- Manage consequences & rewards
- Follow through: Allow all to see the impacts of their efforts (both positive and negative)

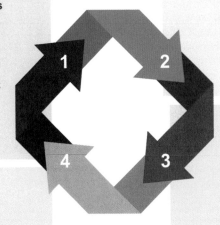

As you'll see in the **Roadmap, Operational Execution** includes four steps in a nearly continuous loop to manage your journey. These steps encourage active management of the decisions and actions that will move the priorities forward and maintain the connection between company-wide (Enterprise) priorities and what's happening on the ground. Like the **Roadmap**, that connection is dynamic. And that makes it even more important for everyone to know their role and what happens when objectives are met (or not). We've included two **Aids** to help: **Responsibility Assignment** and **Consequence Management**.

Take a moment up front to clarify the role of each person or team in delivering on your priorities. Consider the interdependencies—areas where you depend on others (or they depend on you), for important information or activities to complete tasks, processes, etc. Our **Responsibility Assignment Aid** helps you to make those relationships explicit. It's easier to connect people, actions, and decisions to results when everyone knows how things work together.

By the way, it's important to recognize—and share with your team—that consequences can be either positive or negative. Everyone must know (and see) what happens when results are achieved or not. CEOs must define incentives or rewards for success and, equally importantly, specify penalties for failure to meet objectives.

Even with clearly assigned responsibilities and consequences, it can be challenging to make the necessary adjustments. Your team's ability to deal with shifts in your landscape can make or break

success. Agility is the ability to size up the situation, figure out what's needed, and shift direction quickly. It takes time, practice, and deliberate attention to build that agility muscle throughout the organization. That's where our **Agility Assessment Aid** comes in. Use it to assess the ability of your team to shift gears quickly and

> **Agility is the ability to size up the situation, figure out what's needed, and shift direction quickly. It takes time, practice, and deliberate attention to build that agility muscle throughout the organization.**

effectively. The **Aid** considers four different dimensions of agility to give you a better sense of where you excel and where you can improve.

Each of these **Aids** is helpful on its own. They can be even more powerful when used together in tandem. Take a systems approach to incorporate these **Aids** and manage your operational strategy. Accelerate success in operational execution using our tips.

 EXAMPLE

Operational Scorecard

An operational scorecard measures ongoing health and illustrates trends over time.

Operational Execution

Progress as of end of month							
Product Innovation Initiative		**Action Plan Completion %** **(Activity Metric)**			**Progress Toward Goal %** **(Effectiveness Metric)**		
Objectives		Actual	Planned	Difference	Actual	Target	Difference
Team Engagement Practices	Clear and communicated team ambition	78	80	(2.0)	38	84	(46.0)
	A visible and engaged management team	90	90	0.0	65	100	(35.0)
	Empowered employees and teamwork	40	45	(5.0)	1	1	(0.5)
	A structured HR mgmt. process for long-term HR management	40	45	(5.0)	1	1	(0.5)
Multi-Function Processes	First level inspection – line and product	60	70	(10.0)	50	85	(35.0)
	Product quality assurance	55	65	(10.0)	73	85	(12.0)
	Daily operation Management	89	90	(1.0)	85	85	0.0
	Weekly/monthly operation management	87	91	(4.0)	1	2	(1.0)
	Performance improvement and product enhancements	45	55	(10.0)	10	65	(55.0)
Capability Development	Technical competence	70	76	(6.0)	98	94	4.8
	Key technical support	85	90	(5.0)	1	3	(2.0)
	Frontline supervision	45	50	(5.0)	10	10	0.0
	Operational management	50	60	(10.0)	100	100	0.0

Overall self-assessment

To what extent:
- Are we doing what we said we'd do?
- Are the actions moving us toward the goal?
- Does the work depend on other actions, people, departments, processes, etc?

Rating:

Project Info

Project name:	Product Innovation Initiative
LOB:	Data & Analytics
Team Leader:	Joanna Smith
Initiative Champion:	Vinay Pora

Main KPI

	Budget	Actual YTD	Monthly Status
RF – Product Reliability Factor		96.46	
FFR – Prototype Fast Failure Rate		77.00	
Overtime Hours		20.00	
PF – System Performance Factor		87.15	

Highlights/Lowlights	Next Activities
Team vision and objectives well communicated and displayed	Cascading of 2013 objectives to the programmer and product delivery levels
2012 departmental success celebration occasions. Emphasis on All-Hands meetings plus 2 monthly cross team lunches	Accelerating observations and including inter-departmental and inter-team collaboration efforts
The delegation system is working well. 2012 performance reviews based on performance recognition criteria	Ensuring systematic startup and launch (or relaunch) of new (or upgraded) products
Implementing of the HR optimization project completed in December 2012	Definition of target organization
First level outcomes reported in the daily project coordinators report	Identify critical path and share with other collaborators at least weekly
Implementation of the P2 reviewed roadmap	Full implementation of the calibration plan
Each department representative reviewing previous 24 hours performance to the team for correctives actions if required	Ensuring systematic completion of actions and escalation of complexity to higher level
Consistent weekly/monthly product reviews with coding, issue resolution, costs, sales, etc.	Robustness of planning and ensuring prerequisites are addresses
Review of robustness of product and review of the P6 trigger points	Accelerating 'fast-failure' and prototyping
Renewed focus on certification programs	Certification of 2 new programmers in Swift, PHP; recertification of all in Objective-C
Streamlining work requests using collaboration tool	
Call and customer management leadership skills highlighted	
Developers on rotational assignments	

AREAS OF CONCERN + ACCELERATION OPPORTUNITIES – Project innovation initiative project only

Critical streams lag in performance, despite high activity. Adapt action plans in order to meet launch and customer transition goals by end of this year, with limited additional investment. Reallocate or redeploy people resources and dollars. The consolidated action plan to be ready by April 19th 2013.

AID

Responsibility Assignment

A Responsibility Assignment (RACI) Chart clarifies roles and responsibilities for overall work streams.

What does a Responsibility Assignment Chart do?

- Describes how each role participates in delivering the priority
- Focuses on roles, not individuals; e.g., project manager is a role that many people can perform
- It's useful for action plans, products, processes, projects, and deliverables
- Allows duties to be redistributed effectively between groups and individuals

How to perform a RACI?

For each operational priority:

1. Identify the key actions needed in each work stream, process, etc. to achieve the priority
2. Consider the key roles involved in doing the work
3. Assign R-A-C-I to each role
   - Sometimes one role is both accountable and responsible for an action or task
   - Beyond that, it's best to assign just one participation type to each role for each action/task

RACI Responsibility Assignment Chart	
Responsible	The "doer" of the action; can be shared
Accountable	The decision-maker; has power to say yes/no; only one per task or action
Consulted	Gives input *before* final decision/action; promotes two-way communication
Informed	Told *after* decision/action is taken; kept in the loop

When is RACI particularly useful?

- **Workload Analysis**: When used against individuals or departments, overloads can be quickly identified
- **Re-organization:** To ensure key functions and processes are not overlooked
- **Employee Turnover:** Newcomers can quickly identify their roles and responsibilities

EXAMPLE

Responsibility Assignment (RACI) – Operations Priority

A Responsibility Assignment (RACI) Chart clarifies roles and responsibilities for a specific project.

RACI Company X					
Operational Priority – Develop Commercial activities		**Functional Roles**			
Key Actions (The steps in the completion of the work streams or business processes needed to achieve the priority)	**Finance Director**	**Sales Director**	**Marketing Director**	**Business Development Director**	**Strategy Director**
Identify potential new markets		C	C	R	A
Perform full strategic fit analysis (deliver to ExCo)	I	C	C	C	R
Recommend specific segments to be entered	I	C	A	R	R
Develop marketing plan for each segment	I	C	R/A	I	C
Develop commercial strategy for each segment	A	R	C	I	

For each operational priority:

Step 1: Identified the key actions needed to achieve the priority

Step 2: Considered the key roles involved in doing the work

Step 3: Assigned R-A-C-I to each role

Tips:

- Sometimes one role is both accountable and responsible for an action (or task)
- Beyond that, it's best to assign just one participation type to each role for each action (or task)

Operational Execution

AID

Managing Consequences

Manage consequences in a transparent, consistent manner to hold people accountable for doing what they commit to do.

Set clear expectations for individuals and teams.
- *Agree on* the expectations. Formalize them in writing at the outset

Monitor progress versus expectations.
- *Be proactive.* Seek information and input from others in assessing progress and performance on the goal or task
- *Create feedback channels* to assess task delivery or goal progress
- *Incorporate multiple data points.* Use objective and subjective data to get a more complete picture of the team member's performance

Apply consequences.
- Praise, encourage, or reward individuals and teams that are doing well or making legitimate progress
- Understand the source of failure for those who underperform and match the response (or action) to best address the cause

Cause of Failure	Action
Ability: They lack the skills to complete the task or meet expectations	Train, coach, reassign, or find another way to build skills; renegotiate deadline to allow time to learn
Motivation: They don't want to do it	Coach, redirect, reprimand: send the message you are watching
Capacity: They lack resources or time	Renegotiate deadline or priority; add people or resources to help

 AID

Effective Consequence Management

Consider the following for effective consequence management:

Credibility is about doing what you say you will do.
- True for the CEO and for everyone else in the organization
- Holding people accountable builds credibility

Accountability must include balance.
- **Positive consequences**—for meeting or exceeding expectations—earn rewards or praise
- **Negative consequences**—when failing to deliver what's expected, on time and at the required quality—warrant different actions, depending on the cause of failure

- **Failure to meet expectations typically has three causes:**
  - Insufficient ability
  - Lack of motivation
  - Insufficient capacity

AID

Agility Assessment

Agility: the set of capabilities that let you and your team shift direction quickly and effectively.

Operational Execution

Competitive

We actively monitor our competitors' tactics and assess the implications for us — ① ② ③ ④

Our products and services routinely raise the bar for others — ① ② ③ ④

Our ability to learn and adapt gives us a competitive edge, even against larger competitors — ① ② ③ ④

Anticipatory

We anticipate and plan for changes — ① ② ③ ④

We make decisions quickly (and honor them) — ① ② ③ ④

We invest in scanning the horizon, including other industries, geographies, routes — ① ② ③ ④

Adaptive Velocity

We effectively prioritize and manage our portfolio, using aligned budgets and forecasts — ① ② ③ ④

We acknowledge breakdowns quickly, then focus on learning and course correction — ① ② ③ ④

We regularly review performance vs. intended results — ① ② ③ ④

We rapidly develop and deploy new capabilities — ① ② ③ ④

We avoid silos, encourage cross-team collaboration — ① ② ③ ④

Contextual

Our reporting and IT systems provide rapid feedback on operations, letting us highlight changing conditions — ① ② ③ ④

We invest in scanning the horizon, including other industries, geographies, routes — ① ② ③ ④

Senior leaders set the tone and ensure line people can explain how their tasks contribute to larger company strategy and goals — ① ② ③ ④

How it works:

- Rate your self, team, or organization along these four dimensions of agility—from strongly disagree (1) to strongly agree (4)
- Total the scores
  - **Near or above 50:** You are quite agile, likely with structures, systems, and mindset that allow you to use your ability to shift directions quickly and effectively as a distinct advantage
  - **Below 30:** You are at great risk of falling well behind—or failing—when conditions change
- Compare perceptions with your leadership team
- Have a conversation to consider possible areas of weakness; identify specific actions to remedy them and increase your agility

Operational Execution

Operational Execution

Keep an eye on cash — not just free cash flow, but *accessible* cash.

- Financial reporting and operational scorecard should show where cash is really available and what it costs to get it when wanted or needed
- Know where your positive cash sits and and the cost and process to deploy it

Reinforce positive behaviors, values, and results.

- Consequences can be positive or negative
- Too often, leaders focus on negative outcomes and neglect rewards for work well done

Create a safe environment for honest reporting.

- Red indicator is cause for reflection and assistance, not immediate reprimand

Share results broadly via regular, company-wide or general meetings, newsletters, emails, etc.

- Be sure to celebrate success and identify the rough spots

Establish a governing body or group to review your operational execution more objectively.

- Include members from a broad spectrum of disciplines and levels
- Give the group a clear mandate: meeting frequency, review schedule, and rules for reporting or communicating their feedback

Organizational Capabilities Assessment

Managing your strategy journey and getting to the destination requires specific individual and organizational capabilities, within teams and across the entire organization. If you're walking through this book sequentially, you have considered your internal capabilities at least twice: once as part of understanding your **Current Reality** to **Set the Destination** (Section 1); and again, as a key input to Gap Analysis in Section 2 (If not, this might be a good time to look at those tools.). Generally, those earlier tools focus on the Enterprise level view: in what ways do your internal strengths and weaknesses shape where you are today and what it will take to achieve the vision? They also look at all types of assets and resources—people, equipment, relationships, capital, and more.

The **Organizational Capabilities Assessment Tool** focuses specifically on the behaviors and competencies your team needs to succeed. It's about human capital—yet not about individual performance, *per se*. Reviewing your organizational capabilities sets the tone for what's expected Enterprise-wide, for specific areas of the business, and subsequently, also for individuals. Done well and in the context of your strategy, it fixes attention on the most critical capabilities needed to succeed and achieve your vision. Consequently, our **Roadmap** purposely starts with the destination (vision).

Organizational Capabilities Assessment

Look across the team to understand both collective and individual competencies.

STEP 1	STEP 2	STEP 3	STEP 4
Start With the Destination	**Assess Current Capabilities**	**Close Gaps**	**Monitor and Adapt**

KEY ACTIONS

- Link to your vision & critical objectives
- Specify what each role contributes to the success of the team and the vision
- Identify top 3-5 behavioral competencies needed in each role
  - Highlight areas of critical, specialized technical expertise
- Distinguish between collective leadership competencies and those needed for specific areas (e.g., support functions, business development, manufacturing, operations)

KEY ACTIONS

- Review gap analysis from strategic plan
- Assess operating performance to identify areas of strength and weakness
- Use performance management process outcomes to assess individual capabilities
- Highlight areas where change is needed

KEY ACTIONS

- Direct your energy to things that matter most and have an impact
- Identify where you most benefit from internal vs. external input
  - Consider full-time, part-time, or temporary support
- Match capabilities to organizational roles
- Craft a plan to hire, develop, or redeploy talent

KEY ACTIONS

- Review organizational capabilities at least annually
  - Place it in the context of current and projected business performance
  - Incorporate learning and what's changed since the last review
  - Consider what competencies you may need to develop, add, or replace
- Adapt plan to continue building organizational capabilities

More than a snapshot of performance, an organizational assessment also helps you to frame decisions. CEOs set regular intervals during which to assess capabilities as they manage the journey. On a road trip, you would check under the hood of your car before leaving and you'd monitor fluids along the way. In that same vein, start by assessing the leadership team. Our **Engine Check Aid** provides six questions to guide you in doing this.

Next, ask senior leaders to consider their own teams, using the same approach. This provides common data and a consistent framework for considering your organization's readiness to reach the destination. Challenge yourselves to consider positions or roles, rather than individuals. Sustained success of the organization should not reside solely in the hands of a few star performers! We've provided a **Team Assessment Aid** to help focus on the team, and an example of the competencies required for different parts of the business. Use the **Assessing Capabilities Flowchart Aid** to bring it all together and take critical decisions. For example, what changes will you need to close gaps, and how will you get the most from your human capital?

Over time, the **Organizational Capabilities Assessment** provides a good sense of your progress in following through on these types of decisions. Making this a part of your regular management cycle also ensures that you set specific time to align your organization and equip it with the capabilities needed to achieve the vision. It's dynamic—just like managing your strategy should be.

 AID

Engine Check

Assess your organization—just as you would check under the hood of your car before leaving—or monitor fluids along the way.

6 Question "Engine Check" to Assess your Leadership Team

☐ **Overall, what are the three things we all must do to reach the destination?**
(e.g., market intelligence, business development, operations)

☐ **What is the core purpose of the Leadership Team (LT)?**

☐ **How does each role contribute to the LT and overall organization management?**

☐ **What are the top 4-7 competencies the LT needs to lead the organization and reach the destination?**

☐ **How do we measure up?**
- To what extent do we have them?
- What's missing?
- What can be improved?
- What do we need to add?

☐ **How will we close the gaps?**

Organizational Capabilities Assessment

AID

Team Assessment

Challenge yourself to consider positions/roles, not individuals.

It's about the team.

Take individual people out of the conversation.
- While technically, it's all about people, the assessment should consider the *collective* capabilities (or competencies) of the organization (company, unit, or team) as a whole

Start with the destination. Incorporate what you've already learned about critical success factors and gaps to identify which competencies have the greatest potential impact and importance.

Establish what each role contributes to the leadership team, then identify the competencies required.
- Look at responsibilities for each role
- Then, look at the overall team: have you covered everything?

Make this an ongoing management process to regularly review your organization relative to where you are on your journey.

Ultimately, this assessment becomes a key piece of succession planning.
- It includes an assessment of current talent and their readiness /fitness (or lack thereof) for the next role
- It highlights roles that must change

Organizational Capabilities Assessment

Required Team Competencies

Each business focus area requires a different set of competencies.

Organizational Capabilities Assessment

Business Development	Product & Service Delivery	Operations
Competencies required for developing accounts and driving sales:	**Competencies required for meeting customer expectations and needs profitably:**	**Competencies required for providing exceptional decision support and effective, efficient process:**
• Negotiation	• Customer focus	• Process management
• Business acumen	• Process management	• Total work systems
• Sizing up people		• Decision quality
• Timely decision making		• Priority setting
• Innovation management		

All XYZ Company	XYZ Leadership Team
• Action-oriented	• Managing vision and purpose
• Listening and collaboration skills	• Strategic agility
• Technical/functional skills	• Leading change
• Safety	

Assessing Capabilities Flowchart

Follow this workflow to assess your organizational capabilities.

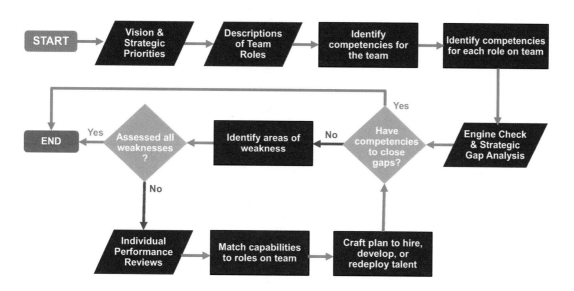

ACCELERATION TIPS

Before assessing organizational capabilities, gather the data and documents needed for fact-based decisions:

- Company vision and strategic priorities
- Engine check
- Current gap analysis
- Performance reviews for team members and other key contributors

Focus on the top 3-5 priorities. Don't try to do everything all at once.

- Do you have the most critical competencies needed to be successful to drive those priorities forward?
- Do you have them in sufficient quantity? Is this a question of capacity or ability?

Individuals on your leadership team contribute differently to the overall company management, in addition to leading their functional or operational teams. These require emphasis on different competencies.

- Very helpful to know when describing roles, creating job descriptions, hiring, and staffing

Organizational Capabilities Assessment

Performance Management

Managing staff performance is critical to effectively balance strategy and operations. Quite simply, no CEO can execute strategy or deliver on daily commitments without people. Unlike the preceding tool, **Performance Management** is about individuals. Good performance management is more than a catalogue of success and failure. It's about creating a shared understanding of how each individual contributes to the effort to reach the destination. Your approach to managing performance should provide a framework for holding people accountable: to what extent did they achieve what we asked or expected them to achieve?

We've included this tool as part of managing the journey, because this process must be both active and ongoing. It's a continuous loop of setting goals, monitoring progress, and rewarding (or correcting) results—similar to what's needed to manage your strategy. The process detailed in our **Roadmap** is fairly simple. Yet the practice of managing performance is much less so. Success depends on the integrity and transparency of the process, how well your organization links rewards or consequences to results, and how much the organization invests in its people. Managing performance is at the heart of building a culture based on results, accountability, and people.

Whether you're managing staff performance company-wide or talking about a specific employee's performance, the process is the same. The cycle presented in our **Roadmap** is equally useful for managing individual performance or defining a company-wide performance management process.

ROADMAP

Managing performance is not linear. It's a continuous loop.

Performance Management

STEP 1	STEP 2	STEP 3	STEP 4
Set Objectives	**Monitor Progress**	**Plan Development**	**Reward and Renew**

KEY ACTIONS

- Start with business objectives
- Describe how the role contributes to business success
- Define success for the unit, team, or role
  - Agree on 3-5 SMART objectives for the person
- Set metrics for reward.
  - Set baseline for metrics

KEY ACTIONS

- Set timeline for periodic review
- Determine how to document progress
  - e.g., evidence, required contributors, tools, etc.
- Conduct performance conversations
- Assess results vs. metrics
  - Meeting expectations?
  - Need help in current role?
  - Need new challenges, opportunities, or skills?

KEY ACTIONS

- Consider current role and longer-term aspirations
- Identify competencies needed for future success
- Select 1-2 focus areas
- Define a plan to develop needed skills
  - On-the-job, cross-team, formal training, independent learning, mentoring, etc.
- Document plan and set development timeline

KEY ACTIONS

- Consider employee, unit, and company performance vs. metrics
- Recognize and reward achievements.
  - Express appreciation, praise achievements
  - Issue special team bonuses or make merit salary adjustments, if appropriate
- Refresh objectives and renew employee performance plans

Effective performance management also helps employee retention. It demonstrates the employee's value to the company and fosters the link between strategic intent of the business or organization, and personal development or career management. The **Aids** we've included in this tool are intended to help make performance management meaningful. In particular, we encourage you to take the time to set truly SMART[1] objectives. It's worth the effort to: ensure clarity, build trust, and link performance to business outcomes. Two other **Aids**, **Performance Appraisal Tips** and **Performance Appraisal Conversations**, suggest what you might ask and how to create a positive experience from performance appraisal conversations. Make the most of your performance management by incorporating the best practices found in our **Aid** of the same name.

> **No performance management cycle is complete without also considering development.**

Good performance management also includes an opportunity to look forward: in what ways do we want our people to grow? Thus, no performance management cycle is complete without also considering development. Performance appraisals tend to be backward-facing—focusing on the actions and behaviors that contributed to or detracted from specific results. Development planning is forward-facing—providing a path to build competencies for current and future business needs. The performance management process helps leaders give people the opportunities, tools, and learning they need to be successful.

Even accounting for learning that occurs simply by doing, development doesn't just happen. It needs a plan. A *good* plan. The Corporate Leadership Council repeatedly finds that:

- Executive commitment to development improves employee potential by roughly 30%.[2]

- High quality, credible development plans that are taken seriously by managers improve performance by another 30%.

A good development plan is achievable with a reasonable amount of stretch, and includes training or programs that build job-relevant networks. Good plans also connect individual personal performance to the organization's strategy and objectives. A bad plan is actually worse than having no plan at all. When they are neither achievable nor actionable, such plans frustrate employees and erode trust in your leaders.

---

[1] SMART = Specific, Measurable, Achievable, Results-focused, Time-bound. See the SMART Objectives Aid.

[2] Initially reported in "Unlocking the Full Value of Rising Talent" in 2005, the Corporate Leadership Council continues to cite this statistic.

Development planning starts with what a staff member wants to do or achieve. Our **Development Planning Aid** guides that conversation so that both manager and staff member can determine what to develop first. Of course, development requires specific actions; it's not just a plan. Not all actions are effective in every situation. That's why we've outlined the types of possible development actions and the core purpose for each. Managers at any level use the **Development Actions Aid** to align the actions with the intended development purpose. CEOs can use the **Aids** collectively to allocate resources for development (e.g. according to types of needed development actions), and support staff in creating and following these plans.

Review our tips to accelerate your organization's performance management approach.

AID

Creating SMART Objectives

	Consider	Example
Specific	What will the goal accomplish? Why and how will you accomplish it? Do both supervisor and staff member have the same understanding?	To improve overall company performance, we need to reduce operating expenses without losing ground with our customers
Measurable	How will you know whether the goal has been reached? Ask, how much; how many? If you are improving something, consider the *'from > to'*	Our operating expense ratio has been higher than our competitors' in recent years and continues to rise in this flat market. We will reduce expenses by 11%
Achievable	Is this goal within your reach? Will meeting the goal challenge or stretch you meaningfully? Do you have the necessary skills, authority, and resources to accomplish this?	Recent review of operations and customer preferences offer several opportunities for improvement. Our team has direct control over operating expenses
Results-Focused	What is the benefit of accomplishing this goal? Done well, what is the outcome or result? (These are not the activities needed to reach the goal) How is this goal relevant to our company mission or objective?	Improved (lower) operating ratio means higher operating profit
Time-Bound	By when will you accomplish this? Does this deadline create a sense of urgency? (It should not be 'easy')	We'll do this by year-end. We'll check progress quarterly

▶ *Example of SMART Goal: By year-end, we'll reduce operating expenses by 11%, as part of our shared goal with Sales to lower our operating ratio and improve profitability*

Performance Management

Performance Appraisal Tips

Good performance reviews start with honest, open conversation.

▶ **DO**

- Demonstrate for your staff that this is also important to you

- Set aside a block of time, prepare for the conversation, and meet away from other distractions and interruptions

- Offer specific and balanced feedback—neither all positive or all negative

- Include specific, relevant examples of situations or behaviors that could be improved *and* that show when the employee has been successful

- Listen actively. Ask for clarification and seek to understand by verbally acknowledging that you've heard them

- Relate outcomes to competencies — technical, functional, and leadership capabilities—that can be developed

▶ **DON'T**

- Postpone your appointment or allow too much time between review conversations

- Focus too heavily on the past. Examples should be recent and relevant to current work

- Speak in hypotheticals or generalities

Performance Management

AID

Performance Appraisal Conversations

Questions you might ask at each stage of the performance cycle.

	Start of Cycle	Mid-Cycle	End of Cycle
Set Objectives	• How will our team contribute to the business goals? • Which goals are most relevant for this staff member?	• To what extent are these objectives still relevant? • What have you observed about the staff member's work?	• To what extent did they achieve the goals? • In what ways will we adjust the goals?
Monitor Progress	• When will we monitor progress? • What's the easiest and most effective way to monitor progress? • What will we do to avoid surprises?	• To what extent are they making expected progress? • What else do they need to be successful or remain on track?	• How easy or hard was it to monitor progress? • Can we see success? • What adjustments do we need?
Plan Development	• What does my staff member want to learn or do next in their career? • What additional or different skills or experiences may help them achieve their near- or longer-term goals?	• To what extent have they participated in training, new projects, or mentoring to build their skills? • What have they learned from that?	• To what extent are they ready for the next step in her role or career? • What else do they need to learn?
Reward and Refresh	• What can my staff member expect if they meet or exceed expectations? • What happens if they fail to meet expectations?	• Have I praised their successes? • To what extent have I supported their progress and growth? • To what extent are these goals still relevant? What's changed?	• In what ways have I held them accountable for the results? • Have I rewarded success? • In what ways will we adjust the goals?

Performance Management

AID

Performance Management Best Practices

Make the most of performance management.

Focus on work and business outcomes—it's not about the person.
- Consider business outcomes and set specific standards required from the job (or role): What do you want that individual to *do*?

Define what success looks like.
- Choose 3-5 SMART (Specific, Measurable, Actionable, Results-Oriented, Timely) individual objectives that contribute to overall business success
- Be clear about what each employee can expect when success is or is not achieved

Provide continuous feedback — there should be no surprises in the formal evaluation.
- Review expectations and evaluations often, as jobs and situations change
- Consider the cause of success or failure: Is it about knowledge, skill, motivation, or the environment?

Involve others, including peers and managers, to gain perspective.
- Ask for and consider employee self-evaluations

Development Planning

Guide to determine what areas to develop.

	What to Do	Questions to Consider
Career Aspiration	• Think in terms of the activities you want to do or how you see yourself contributing to an organization in 2 years, 5 years, or longer • Avoid framing these as titles; this is about a role	• What do you want to achieve? • What type of role do you want to play in that timeframe?
Skill Area	• Consider what it takes to be successful in the current or next role • Choose 2-3 competencies to work on *this year*; include at least one that's needed for your current role and one that's more forward looking	• What do you want to keep doing, start doing, or improve? • What area is likely to have the greatest impact on your current performance? • Is there an area that you absolutely must master (for current or future position)?
Development Objectives	• Define SMART objectives for each skill area— include concrete behaviors/ skills to modify/ learn and by when	• What specific points need improvement? • What concrete results will you use to evaluate whether the objective has been met? • Why is the development action worth the effort?
Learning Activities and Support	• Identify what learning activities will best help you; think beyond formal training • Identify the required resources or support you need and from whom	• What will you do to develop each skill? • Why is that approach most beneficial or appropriate for you? • What do you need from me (your manager)?
Timeframe	• Identify intermediate deadlines and/or objectives • Set time to review progress with your manager	• Are the deadlines realistic, given your workload or requirements for your job? • What intermediary steps do you need?

 AID

Development Actions

Possible Development Actions	For What Purpose?
Formal Training	General training works well for improving employability and preparing for next career move, e.g., degree programs, leadership courses, presentation skills. Targeted training builds specific technical skills, e.g., IT tools, language training, professional certifications. Always look for opportunities to apply what you've learned in your daily work.
On-the-Job Activities	Practical application of new or emerging skills in the field cements learning and connects theory and practice, e.g., project work, short-term assignments, participation in meetings (even as an observer), shadowing an experienced practitioner.
Coaching / Mentoring	Both tap into the expertise and experience of others, typically in a 1:1 setting. These are excellent opportunities to gain perspective about how you do things and how that impacts or influences others. Some organizations offer formal programs internally or through external providers.
Conference / Seminars	Participating in conferences or seminars in your area of expertise helps develop your network, expand your thinking, acquire deeper knowledge of external practices.
Professional Associations	Representing yourself or your organization in professional associations expands your personal network, while often raising the profile of you and your organization. Participation typically allows you to stay current in your field, offers access to resources, and may provide a forum to share your own expertise.
Self-Study	Self-study compliments all other development actions. It can be as simple as subscribing to a journal, reading relevant business blogs, or seeking out subject matter experts, e.g., coffee with a tech expert, lunch & learn.

Performance Management

Performance management is all about the conversation.

- It's a give and take, rather than a lecture, or rating, or negotiation
- **Managers** ask the employee what went well, what contributed most to their success, and where they see opportunities for improvement and development
- **Employees** share what they expect or need from managers to better contribute to the company's objectives

Formally review performance *at least* semi-annually.

- **Discuss** performance at least quarterly: at the end of a project, at each major milestone, etc.
- **Document** key achievements and agreements routinely, especially following performance-related conversations

Actively look for opportunities for new learning and improvement. Encourage your staff to do the same for themselves.

- Books and formal training programs are not the only way to learn
- On-the-job training is the most beneficial and lasting form of development
- Build different skills by leading a project, taking temporary assignments in other areas, or participating in different meetings as a 'fly on the wall'

Keep it simple:

- Appraisal form examples are easy to find online; choose what works best for you
- Always include clear outcomes and metrics, SMART objectives, self-evaluation, evaluations from supervisor and 2nd-level supervisor, and initial development needs

Performance Management

Crisis Management

We all know that crises happen. Often, they are due to factors outside our control.

In Section 2, we described the need to assess risks as you planned the journey. The **Risk Assessment Tool** focuses on risks that have the greatest potential to derail the achievement of your vision. Crisis management is different—and managing risk is not the antidote to managing crises. Risk management is theoretical. It's about identifying, assessing, and mitigating any activity or event that could cause harm to the business. Crisis management is actual. It's a direct response to an event that occurs at a specific point in time. It's usually something that's unforeseen, public in nature, and has the potential to cause great harm to an organization. Yet even then, how the crisis is managed reflects directly on both the organization and the CEO.

One of the most famous studies in effective crisis management revolves around the Tylenol tampering incident, where seven people were killed.[3] While the incident occurred in 1982—nearly four decades ago—the CEO's immediate, very public actions are still heralded as a model for how to behave in a crisis. More recently, Under Armour successfully managed the reputation and brand crisis caused by the lackluster performance of the US speed skaters at the 2014 Sochi Olympics—while wearing Under Armour's highly-touted, specially designed suits. Under Armour's CEO reinforced his company's commitment to the team and secured a contract extension in the process.[4] By contrast, Boeing's well-documented failures with its 737MAX aircraft in 2018-2019 point to exactly how *not* to handle a crisis.[5]

At the time of this writing, the world is dealing with a global pandemic (COVID-19). The systemic nature of this viral event means all organizations have been impacted in ways that go well beyond usual business operations. In this crisis, CEOs and leadership teams have had to consider the various societal structures and tools that underpin work and life for their staff, customers, supply chain, and key stakeholders. The impact has not been limited to a specific area or location of business. And no organization has been exempt from the pandemic's impact. It is still too early to identify the successes and failures in terms of managing the crisis. However, internal communication and each CEO's public response to the crisis are already shaping their organization's ability to navigate this unprecedented situation.

As CEO, it's important to create the building blocks to prepare your organization to navigate a crisis situation as effectively as possible. That's the main thrust of our **Crisis Management Tool**—preparation. Why? Because while the causes of crises vary significantly, preparation for how to behave does not. For example, few people expected a global pandemic to hit with the nature, speed, and breadth of impact that we're seeing with COVID-19.

There's no single roadmap to navigate every crisis, so we didn't include one in this tool. Instead, we've offered four **Aids** and an example that you can use to anticipate, prepare, and communicate during a crisis. Those are the critical actions required to manage a crisis well.

Incidentally, communication quickly becomes one of the most critical and complex elements of managing crises. CEOs can prepare themselves and the team to communicate well in any form of crisis. In fact, communication is the central theme of our **Acceleration Tips**. Master communication to mitigate the negative, potentially long-standing impact of the crisis on the organization. Again, that mastery—or lack thereof—has been much discussed during the COVID-19 crisis.[6]

---

[3]For an overview of the product tampering incident, see: https://en.wikipedia.org/wiki/Chicago_Tylenol_murders

[4]Bruce Horovitz, "Under Armour's crisis management on target," USA Today, February 2014. https://www.usatoday.com/story/money/business/2014/02/17/under-armour-us-speedskating-winter-olympics-sochi-games/5552305/

[5]Michael Goldstein, "Boeing Shows 'What Not to Do' In 737 MAX Crisis Communications, Expert Says," *Forbes*, March 2019. https://www.forbes.com/sites/michaelgoldstein/2019/03/18/boeing-shows-what-not-to-do-in-737-max-crisis-communications-says-expert/#2523772540a7

[6]Much has been written on this topic. This article is an example. https://www.theverge.com/2020/3/4/21164563/coronavirus-risk-communication-cdc-trump-trust

Anticipating and Mitigating a Human Capital Event

Succession planning can be a powerful tool to mitigate a human capital crisis.

Business Unit / Product Line	Current Position Business Title	Start of Current Position	Position Tenure (Years)	Succession Candidates Ideal	Succession Candidates Ready Mid-Term	Succession Candidates Ready Long-Term	Comments
Consumer goods	Head of Division	1-Mar-12	8.3	Head of Wholesale	Promote within department	Recruit	
Wholesale	Head of Sales	1-Oct-16	3.7	Head of Marketing	Head of Sales – Consumer goods	Marketing Specialist	Recent promotion – no need to move for 3 years
Medical	HR Manager	3-Jun-18	2.1	HR Manager - Wholesale	Promote within Department	Recruit	

Tips to enhance people mobility and succession

- *Redeploy talent actively to build skills across functions and areas of expertise (e.g., short-term assignments, lateral moves, and other development practices)*

- *Evaluate organizational capabilities within specific teams to ensure you have the right mix of talent and capabilities*

Crisis Management

AID

Crisis Preparation

Prepare for a crisis to respond better when one happens.

Preparation Tips

Planning

- Identify potential crises that might affect you
- Determine how you intend to minimize the risks of these disasters occurring
- Set out how you'll react if a disaster occurs in your business continuity plan
- Identify business support teams

Updating

- Regularly test and update a business continuity plan
- Create and update an emergency response plan
- Understand your current level of regulatory compliance and monitor pending changes
- Update media training

Common Causes of Crisis

- Natural disasters (earthquake, flooding, etc.)
- Public health crisis (regional outbreak, pandemic, contamination, etc.)
- Technological crisis/IT system failure (including hacking/data breaches)
- Terrorism (man-made disasters), fire, power cuts, theft or vandalism
- Labor or contract issues, loss or illness of key staff
- Workplace violence/harassment allegations
- Legal crisis (criminal indictments, etc.)
- Product crisis, supplier crisis, customer crisis
- Rumors affecting your reputation

AID

Crisis Management—Preparation Process Checklist

☐ **Identify crisis management team members (and other situational experts).**
    ☐ List responsibilities for the crisis management team
    ☐ Maintain contacts for all key internal and external stakeholders

☐ **Document the criteria to define a crisis and when to trigger a crisis response.**
    ☐ Create and launch a notification process to bring together the appropriate internal and external individuals, as well as organizational disciplines at the time of a crisis.

☐ **Set logistics parameters.**
    ☐ Identify a command center for directing the crisis event.
    ☐ Identify assembly points to gather employees

☐ **Prepare communication.**
    ☐ Identify various crisis spokespeople and train them to handle media inquiries and public outreach
    ☐ Develop talking points for executives to promote delivery of a clear consistent message during a crisis
    ☐ Publish guidelines for communicating to the public and the media, including identifying the spokesperson. This ensures that communication is accurate and consistent throughout all channels
    ☐ Set guidelines for social media posting and response; outline policies and procedures for utilizing this communication channel
    ☐ Issue guidelines for communicating crisis situations to both internal and external stakeholders
    ☐ Test preparedness and effectiveness of the crisis management plan and update it as needed
    ☐ Test the notification process regularly
    ☐ Review contact lists, talking points, and regulatory, safety, or legal protocols

☐ **Establish a process for evaluating the response after the crisis.**
    ☐ Document lessons learned
    ☐ Update the plan and notify participants

Crisis Management Team

Establish and mobilize your team to manage the crisis

Before the crisis...

Select the Team Members

- Team leader - Ideally headed by the CEO
- Senior member of Public Relations department
- Subject experts (Product, IT, Safety, etc.)
- Senior member of communications department, media advisors
- Spokesperson
- Human resource representatives

Clarify the Role of the Crisis Management Team

- Analyze the situation and develop crisis management plan to limit impact
- Defend or maintain the organization's reputation
- Team leader: Encourage team to function as one unit

When the crisis hits...

Mobilize the Team

- Prioritize the issues
- Rank the problems based on their impacts
- Seek feedback from time to time
- Double check data/information before communicating
- Act as the boots on the ground

 AID

Crisis Management Tips

▶ DO

- Focus on your response: the way you deal with the crisis is more important than the crisis itself
- No company is too small NOT to have a crisis management response plan
- During a crisis, a crisis management team should be dedicated to managing the crisis
- Be mindful of the use of social media. Information travels at the speed of light
- Don't hesitate to outsource the process to a legal firm or agency who specializes in crisis management if you feel you do not have the expertise
- Focus on prevention and preparation
- Look for ways in which to turn the crisis into an opportunity

▶ DON'T

- Don't respond to everything on social media — stay on message and control the conversation
- Limit the number of people involved— the more the merrier is not the way to go during a crisis.
- Not everyone needs to be involved—stick to your crisis management team members

Crisis Communication

Crisis Management

Take charge of the situation.
- Choose a spokesperson with media training
- Develop consistent messages (internally and externally)
- Look at the crisis from different angles to better understand its impacts and who should be involved

Respond quickly with known facts.
- Social media prevalence accelerates the rate at which information—and rumors—travel
- Address inconsistencies as needed to reinforce the facts and manage perceptions
- Say "I don't know" if that's the case

Be transparent and honest: words matter when in crisis.
- Avoid the "no comment" response
- Don't play the blame game
- Apologize but only if it's genuine
- Show empathy for those impacted and acknowledge them
- Ensure clarity of your messages by avoiding the use of jargon or technical terms

Create a safe environment—internally and within communities—to build trust and foster creative thinking to resolve the situation.

Strong Board Relations

Advisory Boards, Boards of Directors, Governing Boards—oh my!

There are many different types of boards which offer advice and counsel for CEOs in leading their businesses. Typically, the responsibility of the board of directors is to represent the interest of shareholders of the company and, increasingly, to honor its mission (purpose). They review financial performance and strategy, help identify and manage risks, and avoid CEO blind spots. Usually, each type of board includes external, non-management personnel who bring a specific asset, expertise, or perspective to the table. That creates a rich resource the CEO can leverage to shape the vision and drive strategy forward.

> **CEOs get the most out of their boards by understanding their own role *vis-à-vis* their board.**

In some cases, the CEO establishes the board. At other times, the CEO is hired by the board. Sometimes, the organization has multiple types of boards simultaneously. Whatever the case may be, CEOs get the most out of their boards by understanding their own role *vis-à-vis* their board.

The ownership structure of the organization—publicly-held, privately-held, or nonprofit—also influences the way in which CEOs relate to their boards. We've highlighted some of the more important differences in our **Implications of Ownership Structure for CEOs Aid**.

ROADMAP

Your board is not set in stone. Know its strengths and adjust as needed.

STEP 1	STEP 2	STEP 3
Get to Know your Board*	**Agree How to Work Together**	**Size up and Adjust your Board(s)**

KEY ACTIONS

- Meet board members individually
- Understand the interpersonal dynamics
- Identify individual expertise and areas of interest
- Get grounded in board/leadership history

KEY ACTIONS

- Clarify roles and responsibilities
- Set expectations for each member and CEO
- Decide how you want to communicate, including method, timing, frequency, and for what issues
- Agree on criteria for performance evaluation

KEY ACTIONS

- Evaluate current performance
- Identify strengths and developmental opportunities for individuals
- Identify gaps in the collective expertise of the board for current business context
- Establish plan to close gaps (e.g., advisory board, replace or add board members, training, etc.)

*Take similar steps to help new board members get to know you and the rest of the board.

The **Strong Board Relations Tool** provides a roadmap to make the most of a board's capabilities and perspective once it's established. Board composition is rarely set in stone. Getting to know its strengths and weaknesses—particularly in the context of your intended vision and business situation—gives CEOs the chance to maximize the positive impact of the board and to make adjustments as needed to augment critical capabilities. We've included the **Building an Effective Board Aid** to help you consider key questions about the composition and management of your board.

Once you know what you need in a board—and what you have—use our **Board Relations Aid** to build a strong relationship with your board and improve your interactions with board members. Because role clarity is so important, we've also included an example of different, yet complementary responsibilities for CEOs and boards.

Whether or not the organization has an existing Board of Directors, CEOs may wish to consider adding an Advisory Board. An Advisory Board can exist on its own or as a complement to a statutory Board of Directors or Board of Governors. Our **Acceleration Tips** guide your thinking about that and suggest how you might define an Advisory Board's mandate.

AID

Building an Effective Board — Part 1

Ask	Do
#1 **What expertise do I need on my board?**	• All board members need to have the fundamentals of good business management (financial and business acumen, strong ethics) • Add other expertise in specific functional areas and strategy, depending on your business context and to complement your leadership team • Make sure individual members know which of his or her expertise you most value and need. This will help the members find their natural focus areas
#2 How will I structure my board?	• The number of directors should be an odd number to avoid a voting tie • Board should largely be comprised of parties friendly to you and supportive of your vision (to avoid battles in the board room or being forced into a non-desired direction) • Limit the number of directors to a manageable number (5 or 7 members) • Members should bring value to the story (e.g., specific industry, skillset or startup expertise)
#3 **What's the right size for my board?***	A board that's too **big** may: • Struggle to meaningfully engage all its board members • Find it difficult to effectively discuss important issues A board that's too **small** may: • Have limited external perspectives to provide meaningful input on organizational strategy • Not enable the organization to reach important networks for purposes of advocacy, fundraising, and collaboration • Be too insular to provide effective oversight

*Source: Boardsource (2017). *Finding the Sweet Spot*. Whitepaper. Boardsource.org, https://boardsource.org/resources/board-size-finding-the-sweet-spot/

AID

Building an Effective Board — Part 2

Ask	Do
#4 **What committees (if any) are best for my company?***	Standing committees can be useful for larger Boards and to allow smaller groups to work on specific topics in a dedicated way There are four primary standing board committees: • The **Executive Committee** is a smaller group that might meet when the full board is not available • The **Audit Committee** reviews the financial statements with internal auditors and outside audit companies • The **Compensation Committee** determines the salaries and bonuses of top executives, including the board itself • The **Nominating Committee** decides the slate of directors for the shareholders to vote and approve Typically, the Compensation and Audit committees are made up of independent directors
#5 **How often should I have board meetings?**	• Meet with your board based on the frequency of requiring strategic input, or as legally required • Startups should meet more often than established businesses, where meetings should be once a quarter
#6 **How might an Advisory Board add value?**	• The **Board of Directors** is the group of people that manage the CEO and formally approve all key decisions of the company; they protect the interests of the shareholders • An **Advisory Board** is a less formal group of mentors that have specific industry or functional/situational knowledge, and bring their consultative expertise *to the CEO*

*Source: Boardsource (2019). *Do We Really Need Board Committees?*, Boardsource.org, https://boardsource.org/resources/really-need-board-committees/

 AID

Implications of Ownership Structure for CEOs

	Public	**Private**	**Non-Profit**
Characteristics	• Compensated fee and/or equity • Larger boards with committees with independent directors • Emphasis on compliance—Larger regulatory component	• Compensated fee and/or equity • Size of board linked to company size • Majority owners have greater say in board composition • Potential minority shareholders/investors	• Volunteers: Paying members or not remunerated • Mission focused • May have members rather than shareholders or customers
Implications for CEO	• External bodies set many of the rules for how CEO interacts with the board • Timing and frequency of meetings are tied to reporting deadlines • CEO must be mindful of regulations • Board is obligated to protect shareholders	• Ownership largely dictates the dynamic and type of relationship between CEO and board • CEOs choose members carefully. At least a few should be 'in your corner" • CEOs must be mindful of expectations and needs of minority shareholders	• Influencing skills are more critical in managing a volunteer board • Board dynamic is also influenced by size of members' financial contribution, connections, or social status • CEOs benefit from following a consistent decision framework and being clear about how each decision will be taken

 AID

Board Relations

Five steps to build a strong relationship with your board.

1 Clarify roles and responsibilities for the CEO vs. the board.
   - Get input from the board members, and possibly the previous CEO

2 Mind the transition.
   - Don't be hasty in making changes just to be different from your predecessor
   - Listen and try to understand what the board liked and didn't like about the previous leadership

3 Leave your ego outside the board room.
   - The board is a place for open discussions; don't lead board members to your conclusion but let them evaluate/decide on your proposals
   - Encourage questions from your board; don't hesitate to let them know when you don't have the answer right away—get back to them later

4 Listen and act on your board feedback.
   - Honor your commitments and follow up with the good and the bad

5 Build trust through transparent communication – avoid surprises.

AID

Best Practices

Instill discipline into interactions with your board to increase efficiency and effectiveness.

Best Practices

To improve communications
- Make your board meetings about discussions and not presentations
- Communicate frequently and proactively
- Have pre-board meeting calls about specific topics, and/or interim calls (between meetings)
- Send financial information out early (at least 72 hours before)

To facilitate decisions
- Establish a diverse board—by gender, experience, age, ethnicity, and expertise
- Focus board meetings on solving strategic issues
- Set timeline to follow up on post-board meeting actions to facilitate further decisions
- Make sure you know where board votes stand on critical decisions before entering the room

To build social relationships
- Develop a social rapport with and among your board members
- Have as many in-person board meetings as possible
- Ban the use of electronic devices during board meetings
- Allow enough time for the board meeting. Don't rush through it

---

Source: Mark Suster, *"11 Simple Tips for Getting the Most Out of Your Board Members"*, Inc.com., https://www.inc.com/mark-suster/11-simple-tips-for-getting-the-most-out-of-your-bo.html

Strong Board Relations

Extending the journey.

Why have an Advisory Board?

Benefits

- Creates a safe and independent sounding board for the CEO
- Can inspire change based on expertise of the advisors
- Fosters credibility with leadership team and board of directors

Can stand alone, yet is not a substitute for statutory boards of directors

- Properly constituted, advisory boards should complement and strengthen the existing board

Once established, define the Board's mandate and manage meetings carefully.

Mandate

- Focus on specific areas of expertise (e.g., marketing, product development, sustainability), not on the entire scope of the business
- Provide nonbinding but informed guidance to the CEO
- Limit authority with clear responsibilities, sphere of influence, and expectations

Meetings

- Driven by business needs rather than regulatory or legal requirements
- Periodic meetings, or as called on by the CEO
- Often tied to specific business questions or market circumstances

Strong Board Relations

Section 4: Sustain the Pace

Achieving your vision is not a short-term endeavor. Many pieces must work together seamlessly for the organization to be successful. Sustaining the pace is about laying the foundation so that you and your team work together efficiently and for the long run. It takes deliberate attention to people, as well as creating an environment that fosters high performance. Including a set of ongoing activities that support or encourage the connection between strategy and operation will strengthen your foundation. These activities become an integral part of both strategic planning and the operational choices you make regularly.

For most journeys, you set time to take breaks, communicate regularly about progress, and re-energize your team. Do the same for your organization, so that your teams are better able to sustain the pace. We've suggested a few questions to consider.

Questions to consider:

• Do we have a good feel for the pulse of our organization?

• To what extent is our culture enabling (or hindering) our progress in meeting objectives?

• What will we communicate to others, and how frequently?

• In what ways can we use different channels to improve communication and feedback?

• What are we learning about our products/services from our staff and customers?

• Do we respond well to the feedback we receive and take appropriate action?

• How well are we building and nurturing high-performance teams?

• Do we avoid conflict or actively manage it?

• Are we maintaining a consistent pace? Is it the right pace?

How To Use The Tools To Sustain The Pace:

Use the tools in this section at any time to reinforce the foundation needed to maintain engagement and reinforce the commitment of senior leaders and their teams to reach the vision.

Culture impacts overall performance, particularly during times of rapid growth and/or major disruptions. According to James L. Heskett, culture "can account for 20-30% of the differential in corporate performance when compared with 'culturally unremarkable' competitors."[1] The **Elements of Culture Tool** guides you to first understand, then nourish the culture you need. From there, you can leverage culture effectively to support the organization.

The quality of your teams, rather than the heroics of an individual, typically makes the difference in whether or not you reach your destination. Use the **High-Performance Teams Tool** to consider how to recognize and nurture teams that regularly exceed expectations.

Of course, both communication and feedback matter. Done well, both enhance understanding and increase acceptance and commitment. The **Strategic Communication Tool** encourages a critical link between ideas and actions. It can facilitate the connection between strategy and operations, and thus, encourage alignment. Feedback is a powerful practice to gauge how well you are making that connection.

Without new thinking, the threat of extinction, or the excitement of opportunity, it's easy to stagnate.

Finally, the CEO sets the overall rhythm for the organization—the recurring sequence of events, actions, or processes that underlie the way an organization works. CEOs also set the pace in pursuing the vision. Periodically, the CEO may want to vary the rhythm and pace to stimulate new thinking, spark creativity, or allow the organization to take an extra breath. The **Rhythm & Pace Tool** helps you to adjust both rhythm and pace by how you manage the interdependencies, constraints, and resources.

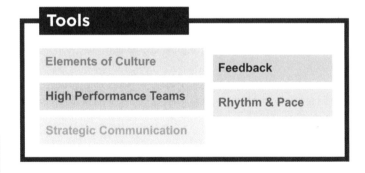

Tools

Elements of Culture	Feedback
High Performance Teams	Rhythm & Pace
Strategic Communication	

> The CEO sets the overall rhythm for the organization—the recurring sequence of events, actions, or processes that underlie the way an organization works. CEOs also set the pace in pursuing the vision.

[1] James L. Heskett. *The Culture Cycle: How to Shape the Unseen Force that Transforms Performance* (Pearson FT Press, 2011).

Dive into the Tools:

Elements of Culture

Ignore culture at your peril.

For at least the last decade, culture has been a key theme in management research, writing, and business conversation. It's often at the heart of talent acquisition and a factor in corporate awards celebrating the quality of the working environment within a given organization. More than ever, CEOs must attend to culture as a key driver of sustained success. During times of rapid change—due to intensive growth or, perhaps, external disruptions—the impact of culture on the success of the company becomes more obvious. For example, as we write this book, companies are grappling with a global pandemic and systemic racial inequality in the United States. Both have clearly disrupted business, the economy, and social structures. A positive culture can be the glue of the organization, not only to attract and retain top talent, but also to get work done and connect effectively with customers. A strong (yet flexible) glue makes it easier to withstand the bumps or sustain an intense period of change. Unfortunately, many of us are all too familiar with what happens when the culture is negative or, even worse, toxic.

Consider these two examples:

• A black Southwest flight attendant shared on social media the story of how she engaged a white passenger in a conversation about race. The man, whom she didn't know, was reading *White Fragility: Why It's So Hard for White People to Talk About Racism* by Robin DiAngelo. That piqued her interest and she struck up a conversation. As it turns out, the man was Doug Parker, the CEO of American Airlines.[2] Mr. Parker was "caught" living his values, quietly and personally. And doing so reflected not only on his character, but also on the culture of the organization he leads.

• On numerous occasions over the last decade, Starbucks has been publicly taken to task for its attitude toward race.[3] And in spite of stated actions and investments to engender change, the criticism and negative behaviors persist. That disconnect between words and actions has made it difficult for Starbucks to shift public perception of its attitude toward race or to demonstrate a more positive, inclusive culture.[4]

> The CEO and the leadership team shape company culture by the choices they make and how they behave.

[2] Brekke Fletcher, CNN.com, https://www.cnn.com/travel/article/southwest-flight-attendant-american-ceo-trnd/index.html June 2, 2020

[3] Ann-Derrick Gaillot, TheOutline.com, https://theoutline.com/post/4192/starbucks-racism-timeline?zd=1&zi=yoq6ojrgxddd

[4] Michael Hollan, Fox News, https://www.foxnews.com/food-drink/starbucks-confront-racism-george-floyd-protests, June 1, 2020.

ROADMAP

Fit all the pieces together to understand and leverage your culture.

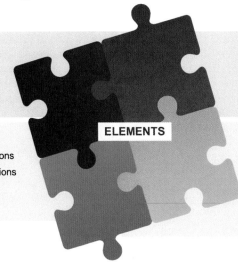

ORIGINS
- Initial purpose of the company (startup rationale)
- History or past experiences
- Institutional knowledge

VALUES
- Beliefs
- Ethics
- Standards

IMAGE
- Internal and external perceptions
- Corporate events or contributions
- Key messages and channels
- Branding

ELEMENTS

BEHAVIORS
- Leadership approach
- Talent management practices
- Interpersonal relationships
- Information sharing
- Consequence management

Use these pieces to describe the current culture.
- Decide if this is the culture you want—or *need*—to reach the destination
- Consider which elements should be reinforced or changed
- Get clarity; everyone needs to understand and embrace the desired cultural elements
- Test alignment; be sure that your systems, practices, and structures support the intended culture

Elements of Culture

Every organization has an inherent culture—a fundamental predisposition that exists with or without a CEO's direct intervention. Those leaders who have instilled a culture of connection and care for their people typically find it easier to make very difficult decisions. The CEO and the leadership team shape culture by the choices they make and how they behave. For example: Does everyone know what happens when results are achieved (or not)? How does the leadership team contribute to the reality of your organization's culture?

Are ideas encouraged or shut down in meetings? Are there clear and transparent 'rules' around how work gets done, performance gets measured, and decisions made? Does the CEO model and honor the behaviors expected from others?

The CEO's example sets the tone for the organization and signals the real culture the CEO wants—regardless of what's written or stated. Failure to define (or clarify) the desired cultural norms typically results in a slew of unwritten rules that can impede productivity or growth aspirations. That's also why we included them in the **Current Reality Tool** as an important piece in understanding your organization (See Section 1).

There are four foundational elements of culture: company origin, values, image, and behaviors. These elements fit together in different ways for each organization. That combination is what makes cultures unique even when organizations might share common traits. That's also why our **Elements of Culture Roadmap** is shown as a puzzle. The CEO puts the pieces together in the way that best describes the culture—they solve the puzzle.

Culture cannot be dictated. You need a culture to which people can relate. It should be attractive to those who must live it. Use the **Culture Audit Aid** not only to assess whether your culture supports your goals, but also to gauge the extent to which your culture appeals to your staff. Once you've defined the culture and assessed its fit with your goals, use the **Culture Advantage Aid** to consider the implications of the **Culture Audit** and identify how you will use the elements of your culture to achieve your vision.

Internal and external perceptions of company culture impact relationships with current and prospective employees and customers. Since we know that every organization has a culture, the key question for CEOs is this: Is the culture you *have* the one you *need?* The CEO gives definition and life to the elements of culture that are apparent—and needed—in the organization. Think about your vision and what you hope to achieve. Use that to guide the organization and create a culture that best supports the company's ambition. Our **Acceleration Tips** may help.

 AID

Culture Audit

Perform an Audit to assess how your culture supports your business goals.

Step 1: Develop at least a handful of questions for each of the four elements (Origins/Values/Behaviors/Image) that adequately represent the most critical aspects of your culture

Step 2: Organize your questions to consider both how well your culture is understood and the extent to which you are living it

Step 3: Rate on a scale (1-Least to 5-Most) how well your organization is performing

	Origins	Rating 1-3-5	Values	Rating 1-3-5
Living and Breathing Culture	Over time, we capture and retain the best elements of our working habits	3	I support our core values	3
	We embrace new ideas while respecting our heritage	1	Our leaders defend our values even at a risk of losing business	3
		4		6
Culture Definition	We understand where we started and how we got here	4	We have a shared understanding of what our values mean	2
	We know how our competitive environment has impacted our evolution	4	Our stakeholders are well aware of our values	2
		8		4
	Etc.		Etc.	

Tips:

- *Choose and frame questions to help you understand whether the current culture supports your future business objectives*
- *Be specific when creating and scoring your culture audit*
- *Culture audits can reveal both the good and bad—points of friction as well as opportunities for synergy. The audit should be a net-positive experience. After all, you're learning about the company's culture and learning about yourself in the process*

Behaviors	Rating 1-3-5	Image	Rating 1-3-5
Decisions rely more on collaborative input than hierarchy	1	The most respected people have qualities that honor our values	4
We manage conflict constructively and openly	1	We sponsor activities that are consistent with our core values	4
	2		8
Our talent management practices explicitly encourage diverse experiences, thinking and backgrounds	2	Our open environment image attracts high quality applicants	4
Our reward system is clearly connected to values and objectives	2	Our customers know and values what we stand for	4
	4		8
Etc.		Etc.	

Culture Advantage

Leverage your culture to reach your objectives.

Based on the results shown in the chart from our Culture Audit Aid.

Consider the implications of your Culture Audit

- Start with the Culture Audit result
- Consider each element *in relation to* your business objectives
- Separate the extent to which your culture is embedded and operating well vs. how well-defined and understood
- Place each element on the matrix based on the audit result
  - e.g., when participants strongly agree on questions about *both* implementation (living & breathing) and definition, the element gets placed high on both axes—or in the top right-hand quadrant
- Discuss the placement of each element *relative to others*, particularly when comparing elements with similar scores
  - What does it really mean?
  - Which one is relatively more important or impactful for you?
  - Which is relatively easier to address?
- Agree (and plan) the actions you will take to better leverage each element of your culture in service of your growth objectives

Elements of Culture

Create the culture you *need*.

Acknowledge your heritage (where or how the organization started)—without getting overly stuck in the past.
- Celebrate the aspects that make you proud
- Accept the parts of your legacy that are no longer relevant or needed—then move on
- Encourage the parts of your history that reinforce where you're headed

Review and update your core values to reflect changes in generational expectations.

Link behaviors to values and expectations for each employee as a key part of talent management:
- Do your performance reviews consider expected values and behaviors?
- Do new hires learn and understand values and origin within 30 days of hiring?
- Are values incorporated into recruiting and interviewing practices?

Reinforce the elements of culture formally and periodically.
- Training or communication about culture is not just for new hires; everyone needs a refresher
- Include your stakeholders and supply chain

Ensure internal and external communications are aligned.
- Reinforce values in all communications
- Share your company history and evolution visibly
- Choose activities that express your values

Elements of Culture

High Performance Teams

The good, the bad, and the ugly of creating and managing teams is often the subject of leadership and organizational development discussions.

Examples of good teams are found in almost every context, situation, or type of group. Indeed, powerful teams capture our attention because of what they achieve and how. Their stories are often inspiring, and many seek to identify the lessons they offer. Two such books, *The Wisdom of Teams*[5] by Jon Katzenbach & Douglas Smith, and *The Five Dysfunctions of a Team*,[6] by Patrick Lencioni, remain among our favorite sources in working with CEOs and executives. While the first talks about what makes teams work, the second highlights things that commonly get in the way of good teams. Together, the two provide a good picture of what to look for in designing and managing your teams.

> CEOs and senior leaders that learn to recognize and/or repeatedly create high performing teams unlock a super-power for their organization.

While good teams abound, high performance teams are less common. High performance teams drive initiatives, tackle roadblocks, and achieve objectives more effectively than others and, typically, with less direct oversight. That's probably why they have become the 'holy grail' of teaming for many organizations. Generally, teams share a common set of qualities that make it possible to work together; we share a few of those in the **Fostering High Performance Teams Aid**. Simply stated: high performance teams do it better. They work together in a more advanced way, embracing more ambitious objectives, and inspiring a deeper sense of purpose and mutual accountability. CEOs and senior leaders that learn to recognize and/or create those kinds of teams repeatedly unlock a super-power for their organization.

Knowing how to build and lead high performance teams is particularly important for lean or rapidly growing organizations. Why? Because those organizations tend to operate with 'all hands on deck.' Staff wear many hats. They have overlapping or multiple roles and line of sight across many aspects of the business. People must work closely together simply out of necessity, and they quickly come to rely on each other to get their jobs done. Further, external competitive pressures create a shared sense of urgency to solve problems or accomplish tasks quickly and efficiently. In flatter organizations, staff tend to feel more connected to the customer or the results of their work, making it easier to see the benefits of good team dynamics.

Our **Roadmap** recommends that CEOs set the stage for high performance teams to flourish in their organizations. Often, that means starting with their own leadership teams. As CEO, it's important to know what stage your team is in right now to influence progress through the five stages of team development. Use our **Aids: Team Development** and **Fostering High Performance Teams** to guide your efforts—not only to create a high-performance leadership team, but also to equip your senior leaders to foster similar teams in their areas of responsibility.

CEOs set the stage for a high-performance team.

High Performance Teams

STEP 1	STEP 2	STEP 3
Get the Right People	**Agree on Ways of Working**	**Nurture the Team**

KEY ACTIONS

- Identify the capabilities you need to manage the team's work (its purpose or objective)
- Assess strengths and weaknesses of members
- Consider the sum of the parts
  - Collectively, do we have the right capabilities? Can we build on these together?
  - Do we have diversity of ideas, experience, perspectives, and heritage?
- Share what each member brings to the team and what he or she wants to learn
  - How can we use our diversity to strengthen our work?

KEY ACTIONS

- Take time to interpret and understand the team's work and purpose
- Set ground rules for team interactions
- Agree to ways of working:
  - Purpose, frequency, and style of meetings
  - Modes of communication
  - Opportunities for learning
  - Timelines for meeting, sharing information, check in, etc.
- Establish tools and systems to ease information sharing and knowledge capture
  - How will technology help?
  - Where will you routinely store/ find information relevant to team's work, expertise, and learning?

KEY ACTIONS

- Encourage and incorporate ongoing learning
  - Use tools that help team members to share knowledge
  - Create regular space (during meetings, in rooms, online, etc.) to introduce ideas
  - Encourage team to consider seemingly unrelated topics
- Regularly and actively consider: What's next? What else? In what ways?
- Remove roadblocks or barriers.
- Set time to refresh and regroup, during the work and when team membership changes

In any team or situation, conflict happens. Often, conflict is seen as negative, but it doesn't have to be. In fact, when handled well, conflict can propel teams forward. At the least, team leaders should strive to manage the conflict so that it doesn't impede or derail progress. Our **Managing Conflict Aid** will help.

Successfully designing and managing teams can be a powerful tool for any CEO. Interpersonal relationships and dynamics always influence the success or failure of a team. Nevertheless, there are specific actions CEOs can take to increase the likelihood of creating and sustaining teams that perform in exceptional ways and at consistently high levels. Our **Acceleration Tips** highlight some of these actions.

[5] Jon Katzenback and Douglas Smith, *The Wisdom of Teams* (Harvard Business Review Press, 2015).

[6] Patrick Lencioni, *The Five Dysfunctions of a Team: A Leadership Fable* (Jossey-Bass, 2002).

Fostering High Performance Teams — Part 1

	What Strong Teams Do Well	How High Performing Teams Do It Better	How Leaders Foster High Performing Teams
Purpose & Values	• Have a strong sense of common purpose and mission	• Clear about and can communicate what their work is and why it is important. • Their purpose focuses energy and drives interdependence and performance • Morale stems from sense of pride and satisfaction that comes from belonging to the team and accomplishing its work; team members are confident, enthusiastic, and optimistic about the future • See their experience together as fun—even if the work is hard	• Guide the team to establish shared sense of purpose and clarity about mutually agreed upon goals • Work with teams to define roles and why each is important to the success of their joint work
Goal Oriented	• Remain focused on the goal. • Embrace shared responsibility. Individuals are committed to doing their part for the team to be successful.	• Embrace team accountability • Possess an innate desire to pursue bigger challenges and produce significant results • Individual team members bring work attitude and ethic that drives even deeper commitment to success and each other, as a team • Constantly seek and achieve optimal productivity; demonstrate epitome of continuous improvement and learning culture	• Recognize team accomplishments, publicly • Acknowledge each individual's contribution to the team, meaningfully • Encourage or enable broader adoption of learning or new practices developed by the team
Interdependent	• Include a mix of skills, experience, and expertise, that are needed in combination to reach the team goal. • Maximize the talents of team members.	• Gravitate toward participative leadership style—allowing all team members to contribute and lead aspects of the project (or work) • Clear focus on the task at hand and how to use those skills to achieve/complete it • Build on each other to constantly get better and ensure value is greater than sum of its parts • Team members feel highly regarded in the team • Able to integrate new members effectively and quickly	• Encourage the use of the varied skills of team members, including those seemingly outside scope of team's work • Respect and honor team's leadership choices and/or identify opportunities for each team member to lead • Remove barriers and/or get out of the way

High Performance Teams

Fostering High Performance Teams — Part 2

	What Strong Teams Do Well	How High Performing Teams Do It Better	How Leaders Foster High Performing Teams
Change & Conflict	• Do not feel threatened by change and growth. • Manage conflict well, as conflicts arise.	• Flexible and agile. Provide rapid response • Able to quickly adapt to constantly changing conditions • Use effective decision and problem-solving methods to enhance creativity and participation • Genuinely value differences and manage them with mutual respect	• Model effective conflict management • Understand and share the rationale for change; these teams appreciate knowing the 'why'
Operating Style	• Agree on operating approaches, procedures, and processes to promote both efficient and effective work.	• Rather than simply creating structure, these agreed approaches enable the team to do their work easily. These empower a high performing team • They have the autonomy, opportunity, and ability to experience their personal and collective power	• Ensure the team has access to relevant information and resources • Guide the team to define their decision-making frameworks • Align the team's scope of authority with their agreed operating practices
Information Flow	• Share information well via clear, transparent, and free-flowing communication.	• Absence of fear. Confidence and trust to take risks, share thoughts, opinions, feelings • Listening is valued as much as speaking	• Model clear and honest communication • Ensure the team has the information it needs (in a timely way) to do its work • Design structures that support appropriate flow of information needed to take fact-based decisions

High Performance Teams

 AID

Team Development

1. Forming (Searching)

Know:
- Members are often polite, looking for common ground
- Some members jump in; others observe until comfortable. Most ask "How to I fit in?"
- Work is typically done independently

Do:
- Identify the team's purpose and agree on goals
- Define team guidelines together (how the team will work, who will lead, when you'll meet, etc.)
- Learn what skills you have and what you'll need

5. Transforming (Reforming)

Know:
- Continuous work teams may establish an even higher level of performance
- Project teams or task forces finalize the team work

Do:
- Recognize group achievement, acknowledging both individual and team contributions
- Mourn the dissolution of the team as it changes team members or projects and/or re-forms into a new team – then get ready for what's next!

Source: Bruce Tuckman, *"Developmental Sequence in Small Groups"*, 1965.

Thomas L. Quick, *Successful Team Building*, 1992.

2. Storming (Deforming)

Know:
- Open conflict may emerge as members wrestle with issues of control, leadership, and communication
- Members compete for influence, with more focus on details rather than issues
- Low trust among members

Teams must successfully work through this stage!

Do:
- Validate differences of opinion and feelings
- Continue clarifying roles and adding resources
- Help team to define its leadership style and decision framework

3. Norming (Identifying)

Know:
- Team begins to work with new energy, dealing with conflict constructively, and seeking consensus
- Individual actions support team goals, based on work habits that support group rules
- Open communication and growing trust among members result in positive teamwork and group focus

Do:
- Encourage participation and professionalism among members
- Allow team to hum

4. Performing (Processing)

Know:
- Team is self-directing, allowing unique team identity to emerge
- Clear understanding of each member's contributions and strengths as members freely share knowledge and adapt to changes or shifts
- Members become more interdependent and loyal

Do:
- Become a facilitator— aid communication *processes* and help them if they revert to a prior stage

High Performance Teams

AID

Managing Conflict

Conflict happens. Manage it to strengthen the team and the outcomes.

Do	Say
Separate people from problems. • Valid differences can get buried in emotions; build on trust and respect • Surface the differences, stressing the need to work together to resolve the conflict, and facilitating conversation rather than directing it	• It feels like we are stuck. I'm hearing you say… • What is the real challenge here? What are we trying to do? What's getting in the way of doing that? • What is the heart of your issue?
Identify and understand the conflict or impasse. • Different needs or interests can influence perceptions; listing the observable and relevant facts helps to get your team members on the same page—everyone knows precisely what problem you want to solve • Declare a break, then describe the issue, establish the facts, and break it down into parts to understand where the real issue lies—and where you agree	• We seem to be at an impasse. What do we know for a fact? What do we *sense* is true? • What do we need or want to know? • What is the question we must address to resolve this conflict? What other questions should we be asking? • On what things do we agree?
Listen—actively. • Each team member should be (and feel) heard, and each benefits from listening to different perspectives • Encourage people to use "I" rather than "you" and to be clear about the issue and their feelings	• Are we starting from the same set of assumptions? Where do our assumptions come from? • How did you arrive at this point of view? • What would have to happen before you would consider an alternative?
Decide how and in what way to resolve the conflict, and by when. • Some conflicts can be resolved quickly, together; others require more thinking, research, or input • Agree who should participate in resolving the conflict and whether it can be solved immediately or offline.	• Is there something we can design together or as a small group? • Can we resolve this right now? Should we take it offline? • How and when will we respond to the team?
Avoid 'agreeing to disagree.' • It resolves nothing and often causes feelings to fester • Explore options together to resolve the conflict—or change the circumstances that caused the conflict	• Help me understand the assumptions behind your disagreement • Which decision model did we agree to use for this? Are we honoring that?

High Performance Teams

ACCELERATION TIPS

Allow space for team members to disagree or air grievances within the team.

- Use your pre-agreed decision model, governance, and ways of working

Reinforce the 'we' rather than the 'me.'

- 'We' focuses on the team; 'I, she, he, they' indicate individual work
- Recognize team effort and achievements. Doing so also acknowledges the contributions and interdependency of each member within the team

Make space for exploration and learning—even if it's simply within a regular meeting. It doesn't have to be an offsite or special meeting.

Integrate new members quickly and effectively. Help newbies to learn the 'secret handshakes' and connect on a basic human level with veteran team members.

Strategic Communication

No matter where you are in your strategic journey, the link between ideas and actions is critical.

That's why we encourage CEOs to balance strategy and operations in a very deliberate way. Strategic communication can be a vital tool for reinforcing those links and placing them into the appropriate context. Well-designed strategic communication helps your staff to understand and embrace the company's strategic plan and business priorities. Ideally, communication also adds clarity and context so that employees can identify how their work contributes to the success of the organization. In turn, that promotes alignment throughout the organization.

As we noted earlier in the discussion of the **Elements of Culture**, strategic communication shapes both internal and public perception of your culture. Often, it highlights the extent to which your words and actions are truly aligned.

Best practices tell us to tailor messages to audiences. It's also important to explain or reinforce the context of the situation. At any given point, individuals will be at different stages of acceptance, understanding, or commitment to what you are doing or talking about. Consider where each audience is as you plan your messages and decide how best to communicate. Incorporate answers to 'why?' and 'how does this relate to me?' Without those, it's harder for people to figure out what to do or the best way to move forward so that they can put the ideas into practice.

ROADMAP

Four steps to develop a strategic communication plan that supports your business ambitions.

Strategic Communication

STEP 1	STEP 2	STEP 3	STEP 4
Set the Context	**Align Message to Audiences**	**Select Media to Suit Each Audience**	**Set Timetables and Communicate**

KEY ACTIONS	**KEY ACTIONS**	**KEY ACTIONS**	**KEY ACTIONS**
• Start with your strategic plan as a foundation for your communication plan • Define the critical themes you will convey consistently, regardless of audience or channel • Focus on what knowledge, attitude or behaviors need to be changed – Relate the context (why) to each audience – Link talk to action	• Identify and prioritize target audiences as the people you need to reach • Determine each audience's level of acceptance • Tailor the content so that each audience can hear it • Focus on context, content, and practice • Create plan to deliver the messages throughout the organization—without diluting them • Construct communication grid/plan	• Choose media or channels for each audience based on: – How they communicate with each other – Where they go for information • Determine who will deliver the message – Senior leaders set the context – Cascade the message, using trusted messengers most connected to the audience	• Relate communications to key strategic milestones for business performance and as things change • Focus on acceptance – Adapt speed and frequency of communication as needed to encourage acceptance – Get feedback • Evaluate effectiveness • Refine messages and timeline based on feedback and evolving needs

A CEO's approach to communication influences the team's ability and willingness to reach the destination. Follow the **Strategic Communication Roadmap** to develop an efficient and effective plan to underpin your strategy, reinforce your culture, and enhance clarity about your vision and the path to achieve it. Our **Aids** lay out the building blocks of communication—why, who, what, and how—and help you choose the media or channel that best suits your audience. We also include things to watch out for during periods of rapid growth, and specific points along the journey when communication is particularly important.

> **Talking only about "why" leaves the audience to determine what comes next. Focusing solely on "what" disconnects the work from the objective.**

We've all heard seemingly endless presentations about why a change is made, or a decision taken. We've also been present when the answer is given without any context or background. Certainly, our children are rarely satisfied with hearing, "Because I said so." What makes us believe our staff will be any more comfortable with this? Talking only about "why" leaves the audience to determine what comes next—and that may or may not be what you really need or want in order to achieve the vision. Conversely, focusing solely on the "what" can disconnect the work from the objective. CEOs—and indeed all leaders—must understand how much time to spend on explaining "why"

before moving on to the "what" and "how." Of course, that doesn't require laying out everything in excruciating detail. It's about setting direction, placing it in context, and providing guidelines so that people have a sense of what's next and when. Use our **Feedback Tool**, which follows next, to proactively assess the effectiveness of your communication through regular feedback and clear metrics.

The faster the growth, the greater the change, or the stronger the external forces, the more communication matters to keep everyone heading in the right direction. Our **Acceleration Tips** include actions to keep top of mind as you adjust strategic communication to keep pace with the intensity of the situation.

AID

Best Practices

A CEO's approach to communication influences the team's ability and willingness to reach the destination.

- Tailor messages to specific audiences and their interests
- Add clarity by linking the current situation with the end objectives. That provides appropriate context so that all staff know precisely how they contribute to reaching the destination, even as the landscape shifts
- Take what you learn about the pulse of the organization to communicate what adjustments are needed so that you continue to make progress
- Be consistent—both in what you communicate and how often
- Connect more effectively with each audience by using multiple channels and media to share messages

Strategic Communication

AID

The Why/Who/What/How Model

Building blocks of communication.

Sample Questions

Why?

Context:
- Describe the destination, including business results and current environment
- Elaborate the needed actions, behaviors, or changes

- Why are we taking this journey?
- What will we achieve?
- How do we make this work?

Who?

Audience:
- Understand the various audiences and focus on the key groups
- Identify their importance to your ability to reach your goals
- Assess how well your message has been received

- Who is impacted? In what ways and to what extent?
- How well do they understand or accept the context?
- What do you want them to do as a result of the communication?

What?

Key topics:
- Identify key themes, topics, decisions you need to share
- Decide on messages across organization— internally and externally—to go from current state to desired destination
- Focus on new or different actions, attitude, behaviors or mindset

- What do I want to achieve via communication: inform, engage, motivate or maintain?
- What information do you need to share?
- What does each audience really want to know?
- What are the key milestones to communicate?

How?

Channels & Media:
- Select media and messenger best suited for each audience
- Evaluate existing channels and messenger used for each audience
- Verify effectiveness of each channel

- What is the appropriate "hierarchy" for cascading messages?
- How do I reach a specific audience like the millennial? Social Media?
- Who needs to be involved? Who can contribute to the success?
- Do I need communication standards (e.g., brand)?

 AID

Media Choice

Choose media based on the characteristics of the message and audience.

Media Type	Interaction	Transmission Speed	Use for:	Characteristics
Print, e.g.: • Email • Memo • Newsletter • Flyer/booklet • Intranet/Website	**One-Way**	**Varies** Dependent on receiver	• Quick, broad distribution of news and other information-sharing • When documentation is needed • Follow-up reinforcement of message • More lasting, consistent themes	• High reach • Moderate impact, credibility, emotion, and information capacity
Face-to-face • One-on-one • Management walk around • Small to large group • Video conference	**Two-Way**	Immediate	• Unsettling news • Recognition • Performance feedback • Organizational changes • Influencing behavior • Checking understanding	• Moderate reach, impact, information capacity • High credibility, emotion, interaction
Social Media • Group • Individual	**Two-Way**	Immediate	• Broadcasting • Efficient sharing • Wide audience beyond intended audience	• High reach, information capacity • Potential to go viral; difficult to control • Mixed credibility, easily manipulated
Mobile Messaging • Text, IM • Voice mail • To group or individual	**One-Way**	Immediate	• Urgent requests/information • Data 'snippets' • Actions • Quick updates	• Low information capacity, interaction • Moderate credibility • High impact, emotion

Strategic Communication

AID

Communication Along the Journey

Communicate at different points along the journey to enhance understanding, increase acceptance and commitment.

4. Change of Direction—Provide clarity about the route and how it still gets to the destination

- Rationale for shift
- Re-energized to continue
- Know how to proceed

1. Start of the Journey—Visualize the destination and success

- Be energized
- Choose to get on board
- How each contributes (my role in the journey).

6. End of the Journey— Celebrate success

- Create a shared sense of accomplishment while acknowledging critical contributions
- Learning and looking ahead (this journey is over, but we're ready for the next adventure)

5. Hitting a Roadblock

- Understand the bump
- Contribute to solutions
- Convey CEO's support
- Adapt timelines or ways of working

3. New Opportunity

- Know how the opportunity fits or contributes to the overall objective
- Integrate into Strategic Plan

2. Reaching Milestones – Celebrate success

- Reboot and re-energize to reach next milestone (take a breath and carry on)
- Focus on learning to be even better through continuous improvement

Strategic Communication

 AID

Communication During Turmoil

What to watch when communication is particularly important.

Not always about 'nice'

Rapid growth is often a balance between extinction and thriving. Be honest and realistic, delivering your messages clearly, even when they may be difficult to hear.

New ways of working

As you grow, you must leverage expertise and information across the organization in new ways. The same is true for communication. Include team or collaborative communication channels or themes alongside traditional cascading.

Frequency

If something's important, it's worth repeating. During rapid growth, it's easy to lose focus. Frequent communication reminds all stakeholders about the destination and the journey plan.

Speed of communication

As business growth accelerates, share new information frequently and in bite-sized chunks to give people time to assimilate what's really changing and what they to do.

What to monitor when dealing with rapid growth or periods of high turmoil

Major external disruptions

When facing lots of shifts in your environment, communicate to buffer the impact and ease the pain for your staff so they remain focused on the destination.

New hire integration

As you add people, focus on communicating expectations. Identify ways for every employee to interact and engage with each other.

Roles & responsibilities

Ongoing change often lessens clarity about roles and responsibilities. Avoid the 'bunker mentality' and knowledge hoarding, by emphasizing transparency as a value.

Control of communication

Supplement informal communication with regular internal communication to squash the rumor mill and help employees to interpret information as well as instructions.

ACCELERATION TIPS

Maintain consistency in your messages, even while varying the media for each audience.

Convert the messages into behaviors and actions, not just words or images.

Balance a clearly defined plan with the opportunity or flexibility to incorporate feedback.

Align words and actions—use your communication approach as an opportunity to build trust.

Repeat, repeat, repeat—it takes time for individuals to process the information and its implications, then to accept messages and build commitment.

Take care in choosing the messenger.

- Close to the audience/known and respected by them
- A direct supervisor preferred if it's 'bad' news
- Directly from the CEO for shifts in direction—then cascade throughout leadership to line management and individuals, following the same themes

Feedback

Feedback matters.

Most of the CEOs we've worked with know that; yet not all seek and give feedback effectively. Feedback is a tool to enhance alignment in your team by pinpointing specific areas for development, improvement, or change. However, it is not simply a tool for individual personal or professional development. Feedback can be used to obtain data from multiple perspectives about all aspects of your business and for different purposes. For example, tap customers to test ideas and understand the extent to which your products and services anticipate and meet their needs effectively. Connect with individuals on your team to encourage, develop, or correct performance, solicit ideas, reinforce your direction and destination, and drive a shared purpose. Or, solicit independent, expert opinion to avoid pitfalls, improve products and services, and test ideas. All of these sources of feedback inform decisions and shape behaviors.

How you seek or share feedback directly impacts the quality of the practice and its value to your business or staff. Before you start, decide two things: what you *want* and what you will *do*. Then match the way you collect feedback (your channel and tools) with your objective (what you want to learn), your type of business, and where your customers and staff interact best with you. Finally, establish a clear, simple process for handling and sharing the data, and identify the best team or person to respond to it. Fortunately, numerous software tools streamline collecting and organizing feedback data so that it's easy to analyze and interpret and to spot trends.

Above all, be prepared to act on the data you collect. That may mean investing time or resources to address an issue, changing the way you work or interact with customers or staff, or scrapping a product idea in favor of something more in line with what your customers actually need. Seeing the impact of feedback—how you behave and what you do differently as a result—sends a message about whether you value the input you request. Often, it makes it easier to get high-quality, actionable feedback next time. And it creates the opportunity for you to say, "You asked for it. We delivered," or "We heard you!" These are common sentiments shared with customers, experts, or staff to indicate their feedback prompted action.

ROADMAP

Obtaining feedback is about learning—and acting on that learning.

STEP 1	STEP 2	STEP 3
Get the Right People	**Agree on Ways of Working**	**Nurture the Team**

KEY ACTIONS

- Identify the key things you want to learn about your business, product, performance, or organization
- Define "to what end"
  - Specifically what do you want to improve, introduce, understand, correct?
- Select the right audience
  - Consider what perspective each audience might offer
  - Multiple perspectives could be helpful
  - Not all audiences should contribute to every request for feedback

KEY ACTIONS

- Decide how you will obtain or receive feedback and specifically from/to whom
  - For customers, draft a target list including current and prospective customer groups
  - For internal feedback, consider whether to solicit specific individuals, teams, or the entire organization
- Choose the tool or channel best suited to gather the input you need
- Analyze the feedback and consider its implications

KEY ACTIONS

- Tailor your response to specific audiences
  - Always be honest, factual, and transparent
- Share information/data and what it means to each audience and overall
- Be specific about what you will do as a result of the feedback.
  - What can they expect? By when?
- Decide how often to solicit feedback
- Follow through

Solicit, monitor, and respond to feedback regularly.

Feedback

Our **Roadmap** outlines the path from obtaining feedback to taking specific, deliberate action based on what you learn. Without those connected actions, it's much more difficult for learning to take root. The **Giving & Receiving Feedback Aid** guides you in handling personal feedback, while our aids, **Successful Surveys** and the **Pulse Survey**, dive into the fundamentals of specific feedback tools. For each of these, we also provide examples—because different tools work better in different contexts.[7]

Giving and receiving feedback—in any context—is not a tug of war to see who is strongest or who has the most power. As CEO, you are also the boss, which can be intimidating when you seek or share personal feedback. You also set the tone for how you'll obtain input from customers or other stakeholders to advance your products and broader business objectives. Use our **Acceleration Tips** to ensure your feedback is meaningful and honest.

[7]See: Sheila Heen and Douglas Stone, *Thanks for the Feedback*, (Viking Press) 2014.

 AID

Giving and Receiving Feedback

Use this aid for meaningful feedback in different settings.

	Giving Feedback	Receiving Feedback
Overall	• Focus on the goal: growth and development of the individual, team, products/services, or customer experience • Highlight both strengths and weaknesses • Frame feedback in terms of the impact of behaviors	• Feedback is a growth opportunity; be open to ideas or opinions • Take time to process the information and reflect—before response or action • Seek specifics and confirm understanding. • Embrace the discomfort
One-on-One	• Understand there is an emotional component to feedback • Shape your feedback so that it includes exploration of how strengths can become points of excellence	• Seek clarity; understand the evidence and the impact • Navigate your emotional reaction (positive or negative) before responding
Groups or Teams	• Focus on outcomes and impact by the team • Consider the matrix of the team: How do the parts fit together? In what ways are they interdependent? • Focus on behavior of the *group* and its *collective* strengths or weaknesses • Encourage team members to participate: it's a shared leadership responsibility	• Consider what can be improved, changed, added, or eliminated • Look for patterns or themes. Test for opportunities in the outliers • Suggest 1-2 things *for the future* that may help the team change or strengthen a behavior

Meaningful feedback takes practice and skill.

Personal Feedback

A 360° Review is useful for understanding an individual's performance from multiple perspectives.

Benefits of 360° Review

- It's **repeatable.** That gives you both a baseline and a clear set of metrics to monitor progress and understand how you have developed over time

- It's **anonymous.** It makes it easier (and possibly more comfortable) for your peers, team, and others to speak freely

- It offers **multiple perspectives**, including your own perceptions and that of your raters

- It's **aggregated.** Rather than having to sort through individual comments, most 360 tools give you a composite view that makes it easier to identify themes for development

Make the most of 360° Reviews

- Consider asking all members of your leadership team to participate in a team assessment. That can help pinpoint ways to increase your effectiveness as a team

- Ask Board members to contribute to your assessment. They are critical stakeholders in and contributors to your success as CEO

- Do your homework. Numerous providers offer 360° Review tools and tips.

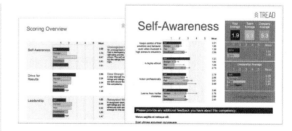

Source: Qualtrics LLC, via qualtrics.com, 2018

 AID

Successful Surveys

How To Avoid   **GARBAGE IN** **GARBAGE OUT**  **From Customer Surveys**

Survey Tactics

- **Notify audience in advance** that the survey is coming, why you're asking for input, and what's in it for them
- **Respect the audience's time**—repeatedly demonstrate your appreciation for their participation
- **Offer an incentive**
- **Ask one question at a time**
- **Time it well** (check the latest research about when to distribute surveys)
- **Tie the survey to other actions the audience may already take** (e.g., purchase, page visit, download, subscription, etc.)

Survey Design

- **Include an introduction** (why the survey and what you'll do with the data) and **a thank you**
- **Be brief**—fewer, shorter questions
- **Ask only questions that fulfill your end goal**
- **Construct smart questions**—mix of open-ended, choice, ratings, and yes/no questions
- **Avoid leading and loaded questions**
- **Use consistent rating scales**
- **Consider question flow and placement** of sensitive questions

 **EXAMPLE**

Happiness Score

A Happiness Score (or a smile test) is a quick way to gauge satisfaction—from employees, customers, other stakeholders.

- *Tie this type of feedback to a specific action taken by the respondent*
- *Use simple visuals to summarize the data and as a basis for analysis*

Source: Trillo screenhot featured in *"The 8 Best Ways to Collect Customer Feedback"*, Giotti, 2018. https://www.helpscout.net/blog/customer-feedback/

AID

Pulse Survey

Take the pulse of your organization or team along your journey.

What	How

• Collaborative, simple data-collection tool
 	
• Tracks the same construct over time, measuring it at least twice (not a 'one-off')
 	
• Short survey (and summary) intended to gather feedback at regular, yet brief intervals
 	
• Used to assess the health of the organization over time, progress vs. a goal or action plan, or the experience of working on a specific project or workstream
	1. Agree on the goal of the pulse survey (what business outcome you will drive) and the specific constructs that influence achievement
	
	2. Set the frequency for the survey (e.g., weekly, bi-weekly, monthly, quarterly, bi-annually)
	  • Consider the frequency with which relevant business metrics or outcomes are measured
	  • Be prepared to act at the same pace that you set for the survey
	
	3. Decide how many questions you will ask
	  • The more frequent you ask, the shorter it should be (e.g., weekly, 1-5 questions; monthly 10-15)
	
	4. Identify the outcomes and drivers for your survey (company practices, behaviors, competencies)
	
	5. Decide who should participate: all staff or a sample?
	
	6. Choose how you'll present and share results—be creative!

Feedback

Analytics — Internal Performance

Analytics tools make it easier to understand stakeholder perspectives.

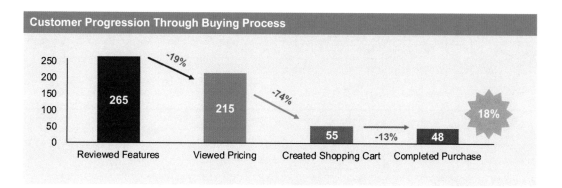

Customer Progression Through Buying Process

Internal company analytics highlight behaviors as buyers investigate your site, features, products, etc

- What percent of prospective customers complete the purchase after reviewing features?
- At what point in the process do most customers leave? Why?
- What might you change to strengthen the customer experience and increase sales?

EXAMPLE

Analytics — Comparative Performance

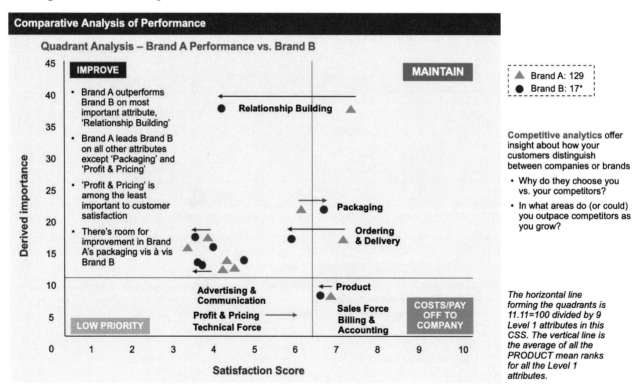

Comparative Analysis of Performance

Quadrant Analysis – Brand A Performance vs. Brand B

- Brand A: 129
- Brand B: 17*

IMPROVE

MAINTAIN

- Brand A outperforms Brand B on most important attribute, 'Relationship Building'

- Brand A leads Brand B on all other attributes except 'Packaging' and 'Profit & Pricing'

- 'Profit & Pricing' is among the least important to customer satisfaction

- There's room for improvement in Brand A's packaging vis à vis Brand B

Derived importance

Satisfaction Score

Relationship Building

Packaging

Ordering & Delivery

Product

Advertising & Communication

Profit & Pricing
Technical Force

Sales Force
Billing & Accounting

LOW PRIORITY

COSTS/PAY OFF TO COMPANY

Competitive analytics offer insight about how your customers distinguish between companies or brands

- Why do they choose you vs. your competitors?
- In what areas do (or could) you outpace competitors as you grow?

The horizontal line forming the quadrants is 11.11=100 divided by 9 Level 1 attributes in this CSS. The vertical line is the average of all the PRODUCT mean ranks for all the Level 1 attributes.

Build the discipline of regularly collecting and responding to feedback.

- Customer feedback advances products (and business); make it easy to collect and share customer comments among front-line, back-office, and development teams
- Effective internal feedback addresses the 'why;' link it to evidence to make the basis for comments clear, and to external rationale to highlight the reason for change
- Two-way communication (with each audiences) builds trust and improves the quality of both data and its interpretation

Strive for symmetry—the CEO role demands that you *give* feedback. Be ready to seek and *receive* feedback about your leadership behaviors from your team, board, and stakeholders.

As CEO, adopt a question to pose genuinely and regularly.

- What's the one thing I might do differently?
- How can I support you on that?
- What am I doing wrong?
- Give me some advice for the future?

Provide tangible feedback visually or in writing to allow time to think and process the information carefully.

Don't just throw the ball over the line. Discuss a plan of action.

- For personal feedback, it's okay to *suggest* a plan, as long as it's used to prompt a conversation and the individual(s) ultimately own(s) the plan

Feedback

Rhythm & Pace

Bob Eichinger and Michael Lombardo identified "Drive for Results" and "Motivating Others" as critical leadership competencies.[8] In our experience, those competencies can also be taken together and characterized as creating a sense of urgency. Faced with inspiration or a threat of extinction, urgency comes almost naturally. For the former, the new and different spurs action; for the latter, it can be a fight or flight response. Absent either of those situations, it can be challenging to keep things moving forward at the desired rate.

In any case, it's up to the CEO to set the pace for the organization and establish its ongoing rhythm so as to maintain momentum and avoid burnout. Consequently, to a large extent, the senior leader's choice of rhythm and pace dictates the organization's sense of urgency. And that determines how well and how quickly the team reaches the destination. Like so many aspects of running a business, it's about finding the right balance—in this case, between too much speed and too little. We've also found that managing rhythm and pace well contributes to your organization's ability to align strategy with operations.

Maintaining a constant rhythm makes it easier for staff to know how each contributes to the whole. It adds clarity. Yet too much constancy can also be monotonous. A senior leader may want to vary the rhythm to stimulate creativity or new thinking. Grounded in a solid understanding of their business context, a CEO considers the constraints and interdependencies that may have the greatest impact on progress. Then they adjust pace, largely via resources. At times, it requires adding energy to the organization by injecting additional or different resources, shifting attention, or letting go of some things that aren't having the desired effect. At other times, senior leaders help the organization to slow down, creating space for reflection or testing and learning—so that teams can actively see the road ahead.

Fortunately, CEOs can readily find tools and approaches that help to manage the flow of work and throughput—two tangible pieces influencing an organizational sense of urgency. Ideally, these improve connection to customers and encourage a smooth flow of information between departments or functions, even while each department delivers on its own commitments.

> **The senior leader's choice of rhythm and pace dictates the organization's sense of urgency.**

[8]See: Michael M. Lombardo, Robert W. Eichinger, *The Leadership Machine: Architecture To Develop Leaders For Any Future*, (Lominger Limited) 2001. Their work has evolved over the years and others have added to and adapted Lombardo and Eichinger's conclusions. Yet, this seminal book remains relevant decades later.

ROADMAP

Manage constraints, interdependencies, and resources to set rhythm and pace. Momentum keeps it going.

Constraints	Interdependencies	Resources
• Ubiquitous and never-ending; you can't always control them • Use constraints to place useful boundaries on what can be done or temper the speed • Remove constraints that get in your way	• Symbiotic relationships or Individual pieces that work together to ensure the entire organization works • Interdependencies are not always immediately apparent • Identify, then manage interdependencies to reduce bottlenecks or improve the flow of work	• The people, equipment, materials, knowledge, or money that create degrees of freedom • Adjust resources to shift course, take risks, or capitalize on serendipity

Jump start your journey:

Create Momentum

Rhythm & Pace

Use cruise control:

Maintain Momentum

Our **Rhythm & Pace Roadmap** describes that process of managing constraints, interdependencies, and resources to set rhythm and pace. The **Priority Assessment Aid** helps you to evaluate priorities regularly so that you can decide which ones to maintain, accelerate, or stop completely to avoid getting bogged down. Likewise, the **Manage Interdependencies Aid** enables groups at all levels to recognize and manage the various things that must work together for the organization to run effectively. We suggest specific actions to create and maintain momentum in our **Aids** of the same names.

Managing momentum is a measured, systematic approach to use energy and fuel efficiently, and for the long haul. Explore our **Acceleration Tips** to ensure you manage those equally well for yourself as you do for your organization.

Priorities Assessment

Review priorities regularly to identify critical adjustments needed.

Overall Priorities

Action #	Action Leader	Name of Action	Number of Staff Involved (FTE)	Targeted Outcome ($M)	Targeted Completion Date
1	John	SG&A Cost reduction across whole organization	4.5	1.2	12/31/20
2	Liz	Consolidate Departments A and B	3	0.8	4/15/20
3	Anne	Launch new product XYZ by Q3	10	6	9/15/21
4	Jack	Upgrade of main production tool	6.5	2.1	6/30/21
		Total:	**24**	**10.1**	

How many people are involved relative to progress or outcomes achieved?

Rhythm & Pace

Actual Outcome YTD ($M)	Revised Outcome ($M)	Estimated Completion Date	Status	Comment	Decision Needed
0.7	1	12/31/20	🔘	1.2 target might be at risk	Need push across organization
0.4	0.85	4/15/20	🔘	On target to reach full savings	
-1.5	4	9/30/20	⚫	Still under development. Added a few resources (+2) to keep launch date the same	Return on investment is now lower. Decision needed as to Go/No Go
1.1	2	6/30/20	⚫	On track for savings	Attempt to reduce key people involved
0.7	7.85				

Will we still deliver what we intended to deliver? Do we alter momentum?

Where are we now? Current Assessment

Should we change course, adjust resources or constraints, or manage interdependencies?

AID

Managing Interdependencies

Interdependencies are those parts, activities, functions, jobs, systems, or processes that must work together effectively to achieve the objectives.

Identify interdependencies	Consider to what extent	Manage interdependencies
• For what critical things does my/our work depend on others? • For what critical things do others depend on us?	• Have we asked for these things? • Do others know why these are important to our work? To the entire organization? • Have we all articulated how each part contributes to meeting the objective of delivering our product, service, value, etc.? • Are we providing what others need in a timely way?	• In what ways do we adjust timelines, systems, processes to improve the way these critical things work together? • What additional data or information do we need to understand and monitor these things—proactively and in advance? • How often do we follow up or check in with others? • Who will be responsible for monitoring how all the parts work together?

Rhythm & Pace

 AID

Create Momentum

Suggested Actions	How
Develop Goals as a team and communicate progress to the team	• Have your team sit down with you to develop goals, creating buy-in and a collective commitment • As you and your team get closer to hitting these goals make sure that everyone is aware of the progress • No one wants to let down the team; this will create a level of personal commitment motion
Focus on the short and medium term	• Ask yourself what you can do today, tomorrow, and next week to get a win? • Have a daily plan of actions; for example, make two extra sales call every day
Break down goals into manageable and actionable wins	• Multiple small or individual wins will eventually lead to bigger wins • If your goal is to be the leader in your sector on a national level, start with achieving your goal on a regional level
Celebrate small victories	• Even if these wins are deemed small, look for opportunities to celebrate them • Define team expectations in advance as to what outcomes are acceptable results • What specific success do you want to achieve today, tomorrow, and next week?
Create a sense of urgency	• Draw the picture of what if we don't succeed, to create the sense of urgency • Get working on your plan now: start small, focus on completing one thing at a time, get it done and move on to the next

Rhythm & Pace

 AID

Maintain Momentum

Shift to a longer-term mindset to maintain momentum.

Suggested Actions	How
Give public recognition and praise to create a company culture of winning	• Let employees know personally • Reinforce positive actions to build overall confidence • Doing this publicly may spur healthy, friendly competition among team members
Pick the right time to challenge the team	• While it is important to challenge your team on a regular basis, challenging them when the level of confidence is high will keep them committed and motivated
Measure Progress	• Look back at what has been achieved so far, including all small wins, rather than on what's left to achieve • Keep track of past successes and make them visible
Embed	• Identify replicable processes that can fundamentally change the rhythm and pace of performance and decision making in the organization • Use these to look beyond the strategic choices and daily initiatives to understand and effect the way the organization works • Find, then manage, the 'hum' of your business engine—key to sustaining momentum
Support the process of employees finding the "what's in it for me"	• Support your team in identifying the "why they need to move forward" and how it benefits them. • Managers should not assume employees know why the company should operate differently in the future
Expect bumps on the road	• Not everything that you are doing will work perfectly. When something doesn't work, evaluate it, and take corrective action—sometimes it means making adjustments along your journey
Remember to have fun	• Maintaining the momentum can be exhausting if you don't take the time to have fun—schedule company events to celebrate milestones

Rhythm & Pace

ACCELERATION TIPS

Be consistent. Too-frequent changes in direction typically reduce clarity and cause you to run out of steam.
- Learn from the past and your progress to make necessary, periodic adjustments
- Reward yourself and the team for staying the course (as appropriate), particularly when confronted with resistance

Find the right amount of "stretch" for yourself and the organization.
- Sometimes giant steps allow giant leaps forward; at other times, it leaves a hole that actually takes you backward
- Avoid biting off more than you can chew for extended periods; it's simply not sustainable
- Adjust the "tension" in the stretch to allow forward motion, without too much loss of velocity
- Don't wait to celebrate until the goal is met or the "to-do" list is complete

Take time to recharge your batteries.
- Don't expect your energy to continue effortlessly and endlessly
- Set aside some time on a regular basis (monthly or quarterly) to take a breath
- Taking care of yourself—and encouraging your leadership team to do the same—is key to sustaining the rhythm and pace of your journey
- Acknowledge the small wins along the way to the bigger goal

Surround yourself with positive people and spend time with them.
- Negativity drains energy and impedes momentum

Section 5: Reach Your Destination

Many navigation systems include a checkered flag to mark the destination. In business, it's not always crystal clear that you've fully reached your destination. Conditions constantly change and you adapt on the fly to deal with the changes. Typically, that means rebalancing resources and shifting operational priorities to achieve your strategic objectives. CEOs regularly consider whether the initial vision remains relevant and within reach. The CEO then determines whether to maintain course or modify the plan. Sometimes, they reset the destination completely.

> **CEOs regularly consider whether the initial vision remains relevant and within reach.**

Having achieved your vision—the destination—it makes sense to celebrate what's been accomplished. Take time to reflect on the previous journey, review your successes, and describe the lessons you've learned. These activities help your organization to identify what changes—to resources, equipment, technology, processes, or people—you need in order to move forward productively and with renewed energy to achieve a new or refreshed vision.

As you reflect on what you've achieved and how you got here, consider a broad range of questions such as the ones below to strengthen your ability to manage the connection between strategy and operations going forward.

Questions to consider:

- **To what extent does our current vision remain relevant?**
- **What do we need to cross the finish line?**
- **How do we thank the people that contributed to the effort?**
- **How will we make the celebration and subsequent review more authentic?**
- **How, when, and with whom do we celebrate success (customers, employees, board, etc.)?**
- **What have we learned? What might we improve or avoid next time?**
- **Who among the core team members emerged as potential leaders?**
- **What are the most critical things we must do to improve organizational readiness?**
- **What is new and/or different about the next initiative or objective?**

How To Use The Tools When You Reach Your Destination:

The **Vision Accomplished Tool** is useful whenever you want to assess the continued relevance of your current destination. When you deem the vision accomplished, thank and appreciate all the people—including partners, collaborators, and stakeholders—who have contributed to your success to date. That's your victory lap.

In our experience, executing strategy with a shared sense of urgency can be exhausting for the organization—even when it's done well. Further, a constant stream of "new and improved" versions of the same strategic initiative typically lack the power to inspire the organization. Thus, before immediately launching a new vision and strategy, use the **What We Have Learned Tool** to consider what contributed most to your success and the things that got in your way. Identify the critical improvements so that you know where and how you'll invest to reinforce or accelerate progress.

Next, consider **Retooling**. Take stock of your organization's readiness to pursue a new or refreshed destination. Incorporate your knowledge of the external forces impacting your business to understand the urgency with which you must retool. Depending on your business, retooling may require investment in or retirement of more tangible items, like equipment, facilities, or systems. All businesses will need to address capabilities, ways of working, processes, and the capacity of the team to take on new initiatives. As needed, return to tools in earlier sections to define how you will align strategy and operations to close gaps—or retool—in preparation for the next adventure.

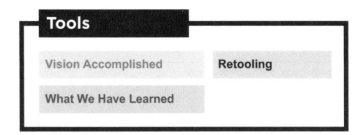

Dive into the Tools:

Vision Accomplished

Thanks to a film of the same name, "Are we there yet?" became a popular refrain in the early 2000s. Since then, it's become a metaphor for endeavors that have lost their luster or whose reason is no longer clear. That sentiment—of the journey that seems to take forever amid the extreme impatience of the travelers—can be felt in all kinds of organizations.

There are many valid reasons why a journey takes longer than expected: changing conditions, new information or learning, unexpectedly high competitive intensity, insufficient resources, or a degree of stretch that's simply too great for the business to reach. Rather than allowing an endless, demotivating trek toward the destination, CEOs must also answer the question: "Are we there yet?"

As we've said throughout this book, strategy is the set of decisions and actions that get you to your vision. As such, strategy requires constant attention and adjustments as things change. The organization benefits from taking a moment to affirm the destination, then clarifying its strategy. That better positions your team to capitalize on opportunities and adapt to what it has learned along the way. Managed well, many organizations respond positively to these kinds of adjustments. Yet, when this happens too frequently or for too long a time, it can also become exhausting. Thus, it's important for CEOs to know when to declare the destination has been reached—or is close enough that the time is right to reset.

Don't we all wish we had a business GPS to show the route, highlight key decisions, and tell us when we've arrived?

---

[1]*Are we there yet?* Film directed by Brian Levant, Released January 21, 2005. Spawned a TV series of the same name and featuring the same characters on TBS in 2010 and a sequel film, "Are we done yet?" in 2007. https://www.imdb.com/title/tt0368578/

ROADMAP

Don't we all wish we had a business GPS to tell us when we've arrived?

Along the journey, CEOs decide what buttons to press: Stop guidance, resume journey, add a stop, or set a new destination

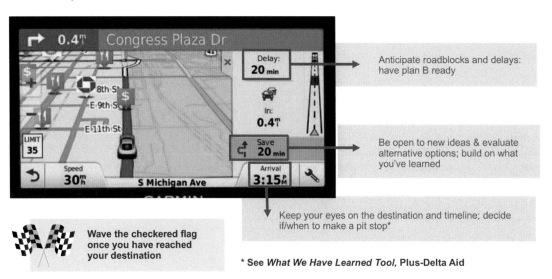

Anticipate roadblocks and delays: have plan B ready

Be open to new ideas & evaluate alternative options; build on what you've learned

Keep your eyes on the destination and timeline; decide if/when to make a pit stop*

Wave the checkered flag once you have reached your destination

* See *What We Have Learned Tool,* Plus-Delta Aid

Vision Accomplished

Using the familiar visual of a GPS, our **Vision Accomplished Roadmap** highlights a few key steps to take as you read the signs and determine whether to declare your vision accomplished. Most of the time, it's a CEO's judgment call. Furthermore, the contradiction of doggedly pursuing the destination and constantly adapting the route makes it even more critical to communicate when you've determined it's the end of the journey. At the start of this we likened that decision—and related communication—to waving the checkered flag for the organization. The **Checkered Flag Aid** offers a decision flow you can use repeatedly to check progress and determine whether it's time to wave the flag. If not, the **Aid** helps you continue as planned, adapt course, or set a new direction.

In our experience, achieving the vision is rarely (if ever) an individual effort. As CEO, you have the honor of acknowledging all those who have contributed to the organization's success. At the risk of extending that racing—and journey—metaphor just a little too far, we've also included a **Victory Lap Aid**. It's all about recognizing what you achieved, the challenges you met, and the people who contributed. For the senior leaders with whom we've worked, thanking people and celebrating success are among the most rewarding parts of their job. There is always something to celebrate and people to thank—even if you don't fully achieve the vision. At the very least, the effort, commitment, and lessons learned are worth acknowledging. Taking the time to do so also bolsters the organization, making it easier—and more compelling—to participate actively in achieving the next vision.

> There is always something to celebrate and people to thank—even if you don't fully achieve the vision.

Our **Acceleration Tips** encourage you to involve others in taking the decision about whether you've reached the destination and in celebrating success. Leaders with strong emotional intelligence tend to see things positively. So even if you didn't achieve your vision in the way you intended, declaring "Vision accomplished!" helps prepare the way for the entire organization to learn from the experience. With the "Vision accomplished!" declaration, the leader also acknowledges the positive things the team achieved, recognizing that no journey is truly 'all bad' or 'all good.' That openness and acknowledgement can improve overall performance—particularly as you learn, then adapt and retool to achieve a new objective.

AID

Checkered Flag Review

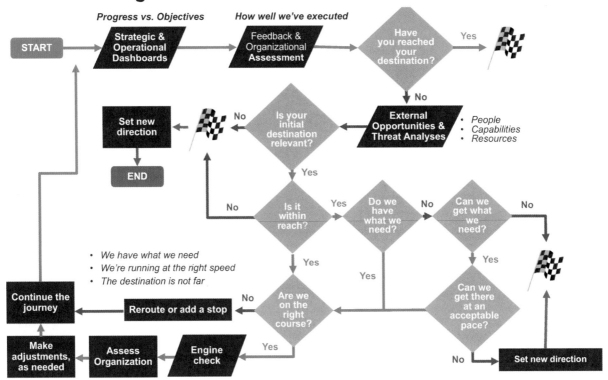

Vision Accomplished

Progress vs. Objectives

START → **Strategic & Operational Dashboards** → *How well we've executed* **Feedback & Organizational Assessment** → **Have you reached your destination?** — Yes →

No ↓

External Opportunities & Threat Analyses
- *People*
- *Capabilities*
- *Resources*

→ **Is your initial destination relevant?** — No → **Set new direction** → **END**

Yes ↓

Is it within reach? — Yes → **Do we have what we need?** — No → **Can we get what we need?** — No →

No ← (back to Is your initial destination relevant?)

Yes ↓
- *We have what we need*
- *We're running at the right speed*
- *The destination is not far*

Are we on the right course?

No → **Reroute or add a stop** → **Continue the journey**

Yes ↓

Engine check → **Assess Organization** → **Make adjustments, as needed**

Can we get there at an acceptable pace? — Yes

No → **Set new direction**

 AID

Victory Lap

Take a victory lap to reflect on the journey and celebrate your achievements.

What Goes Into Your Victory Lap

1. Acknowledge:
- What you achieved
- How you got there
- Who contributed to the journey

2. Celebrate:
- With your leadership team and stakeholders (Board, customers, suppliers, community, etc.)
- Key individual contributions
- Team efforts
- Standout performances or milestones

3. Communicate:
- Company values as the foundation for celebration
- Achievements in market leadership
- What's next

ACCELERATION TIPS

Engage your leadership team in the decision to confirm you've sufficiently reached the destination.

- They provide insight and data to support a fact-based decision

Consider ending your strategic journey the same way you began.

- If you kicked this off with an event, consider ending it that way, too
- Make this a *formal* opportunity to acknowledge individual, team, and organization-wide effort; include all stakeholders in that recognition
- Celebrate the learning and how you'll capitalize on that during the next journey

Strive to see things positively regardless of the outcome.

- You've achieved the vision on your own
- Another event precipitated the journey's end
- Your aspirations exceeded your abilities

Vision Accomplished

What We Have Learned

Upon achieving your vision, waving the checkered flag is only part of the CEO's role. The opportunity to learn and grow is a major outcome of any meaningful initiative—regardless of whether you succeed or fail in reaching the vision.

 ROADMAP

Between strategic journeys, capitalize on what you've learned—the good and the bad.

Learn from failures
- What could you do differently to change the outcome?
- How can you better anticipate failure points?
- How will you know when to call it quits?

+

Identify and agree on critical improvements
- Which improvements are likely to be most impactful going forward?
- Where and how much will you invest to reinforce/accelerate progress?
- Who will be responsible for implementing improvements? By when?

+

Embed what went well
- How will you replicate success?
- Which behaviors, habits, processes, and metrics will be most valuable going forward?
- How will you incorporate these into your operating framework?

 **Build the foundation for your next strategic journey**

Once the initiative is complete, it's important to deliberately set aside time to reflect and identify what you've learned—including the good, the bad, and the ugly. Our **Roadmap** highlights three critical steps needed to build the foundation for subsequent strategic journeys.

Taking time to reflect helps learning. Then use a structured approach to articulate what's been learned and the implications of that learning for the future. While acknowledging what didn't work is essential (particularly if the destination was not fully achieved), it's not everything. To be clear: learning is not an indictment of past performance. Rather, *ongoing* learning is critical for both strategy and operations. It should be forward looking—identifying how you will build on the past to enhance the foundation for your success and avoid or diminish potential pitfalls along the way. Much has been written about how to cultivate a culture of learning. We have shared **Key Resources** that we've found to be helpful in capitalizing on the lessons you learn and benefiting from that effort.

You may have heard of a Plus-Delta evaluation.[2] That's a common methodology used in continuous improvement programs to understand specifically what worked well, what you want to keep or repeat, and what can be improved (the "delta"). Our simple **Plus-Delta Aid** will help you conduct that type of evaluation and capture what's been learned. From there, you can define and share best practices that you've developed, as well as steps to alleviate risks or challenges you may encounter next time.

A **Post-Project Audit** is another **Aid** to learn from the experience. An audit differs from the Plus-Delta evaluation in two ways. The audit is often more structured and formal, evaluating specific aspects of the program. It also leverages other processes and people—often those who were not directly involved in the work itself. Our **Post-Project Audit Aid** focuses on the common sources of resistance to participating in an audit and suggests ways to mitigate that resistance.

To be clear, while learning for learning's sake can be intellectually stimulating and fun for many, its real value comes from what you do as a result of what you've learned. That's how you embed the lessons and capture the return on time invested. It's also a key motivator for your teams to participate actively and meaningfully in the process. Thus, whatever method(s) you choose to capture lessons learned must also include action. Identify specific steps to fix what's broken, embed what's helpful, and accelerate progress next time. Be sure to include a timeline for follow up and hold people accountable for bringing that learning to life in concrete ways for your organization. Our **Acceleration Tips** can help.

---

[2] See IGI Global (an international academic publisher and partner to leading research and academic institutions) for a brief explanation of the Plus Delta Evaluation: https://www.igi-global.com/dictionary/use-story-building-online-group/22865

Learning Culture — Key Resources

Understand and cultivate a culture of learning by tapping into a variety of resources.

Purpose	Tools & Resources
Understand the fundamentals of a learning organization and obtain practical tools to embed learning in your organization	Peter Senge, *The Fifth Discipline: The Art and Practice of the Learning Organization*, Doubleday/Currency, 1990.
Evaluate whether your organization has the three building blocks of a learning organization	David A. Garvin, Amy C. Edmondson, and Francesca Gino, Is Yours a Learning Organization? *Harvard Business Review*, 3/2008. https://hbr.org/2008/03/is-yours-a-learning-organization
Build a culture of learning for your team and organization	Tomas Chamorro-Premuzic and Josh Bersin, 4 Ways to Create a Learning Culture on Your Team, *Harvard Business Review* Blog, 7/12/2018. https://hbr.org/2018/07/4-ways-to-create-a-learning-culture-on-your-team
Learn about two approaches to capitalize on the lessons you learn and benefit from that effort	Mark White and Alison Cohan, *A Guide to Capture Lessons Learned,* The Nature Conservancy https://www.conservationgateway.org/ConservationPlanning/partnering/cpc/Documents/Capturing_Lessons_Learned_Final.pdf

AID

Plus-Delta — Part 1

Take time to reflect, learn, and improve.

Plus Delta Evaluation

- A **Plus Delta Evaluation** is a common tool used in continuous improvement processes.
  - Use it to *assess what your team or organization did well* in reaching its destination and what you could improve on the next journey
  - *Capture your streng*ths, or the things you want to repeat or retain under a "plus" column
  - Use the delta (Δ)—the Greek symbol for change—to indicate items you'd like to change before or during the next adventure
- Take time to structure the exercise and create a comfortable atmosphere to get the best result
  - Make it a safe space, free of judgment
  - Welcome ideas and comments that are honest, constructive, and open-minded
  - Include a variety of people who participated in the effort.
  - Consider using a facilitator who has not been directly involved or connected to the team

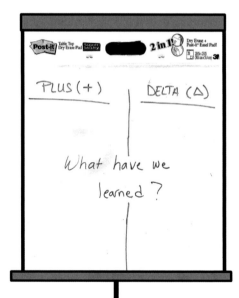

Plus-Delta — Part 2

Start with broad, open-ended questions to stimulate thinking.

Typical Questions

- What was the most important part of the journey?
- What made it harder to travel?
  - How might we fix that?
- What seemed to work well for us?
- What is the one thing we learned that we'd like to take with us on the next journey?
- What surprised us the most?
- What could we do to better manage roadblocks or speed bumps?
  - How do we avoid them altogether?

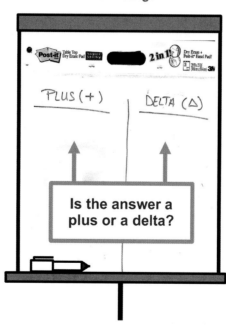

 AID

Plus-Delta — Part 3

Drill down to identify what you will *do* as a result of this learning.

Create a Plan

Capitalize on the Learning:

- What actions will we take? By when?
- Who will be accountable for follow-up?
- What resources or tools will we cultivate or develop?
- Who else needs to be involved?
- What will we tell others about what we've learned?

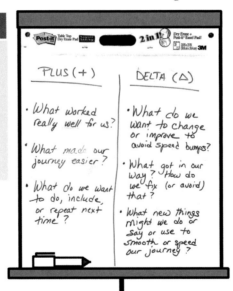

AID

Post Project Audit — Overcoming Resistance

Common Sources of Resistance	Mitigation Steps
Too time consuming	• Make it easy for team members to provide input, using simple electronic tools or a survey that take a short time to complete • Use a simple collaboration or survey tool that combines the inputs and provides basic analysis • Be clear up front about expectations for how long the team will spend on this, particularly for group meetings
They don't know what they're talking about	• Get the right people to participate; identify those who can contribute solely via data gathering and inputs vs. those needed for joint conversation and/or analysis • Include people who had meaningful roles in the project or journey and represent a broad spectrum of types of work and participants, particularly for face-to-face discussion • Invite those with fringe roles in the project to contribute to specific areas or questions as needed
It's no longer relevant	• Audit the journey at periodic intervals (e.g., upon achieving milestones), rather than solely upon reaching the objective • Conduct the end-of-journey audit within a short time of reaching the objective (e.g., when the last big milestone is/was achieved)
It's not fact-based	• Use a Web-based collaboration tool to ease access to hard data
It's just another blame game	• Ask an independent, neutral party (e.g., an internal auditor) to lead the review • Separate managers and staff for discussions to allow free-flow • Build trust by demonstrating faith in the participants and the process, and by managing leaders' reactions to the results

What We Have Learned

What We Have Learned

Learning at the end of a major strategic initiative is far easier when you've already established a learning culture in your organization.

Don't save all the learning for the end.

- Quick reviews done at major milestones support continuous learning and can have a great positive impact on motivation

---

Encourage people to speak freely and offer solutions, in addition to focusing on problems or challenges.

Focus on the 'why' and 'how.'

Make your own ongoing learning visible to others.

- Share a book you've read
- Set aside time in regular meetings to allow others to share something they've learned
- Inquire about what others have learned from participation in external events or programs
- Create discussion areas or break rooms that foster communication beyond the board room or executive offices

---

Make learning fun.

Retooling

Whether you've traveled systematically through the entire book, popped in part way through, or recently declared your vision accomplished—you've covered a lot of ground. Most likely, the same is true for your organization or team. In our experience, the more intense the effort, the harder it is to shift gears. People can also feel a bit of a letdown as they shift pace from the energy and excitement of pursuing and completing a strategic initiative to the more regular rhythm of daily work. You may have heard that called "Initiative Fatigue."

In our experience, it's not only equipment or machines, but also people who benefit from downtime.[3] Some people need more time to refresh their brains and recharge their batteries than others—and that time is a good investment, not only for the individuals, but also for the overall organization. It's hard to go immediately from one major initiative to the next. Typically, a break allows us to refresh our thinking, inject new perspectives, or enhance clarity about our work and how we contribute to success. Plus, that renewed energy can be contagious, which helps revitalize many other connections within your organization—and improves productivity.[4]

> **Taking a break from the frenetic pace toward the vision can and should include time to assess your organizational readiness and appetite for a new initiative or strategic journey.**

We recommend taking a breath while also shaping the next adventure. That retains momentum without exhausting the organization. And it often gives the team a new burst of adrenaline, and something exciting to anticipate. That concept is at the heart of **Retooling**.

Most likely, your business environment and your team have changed dramatically since the start of your last strategic journey. The extent of that change informs whether you simply raise the bar in its current context or define an entirely new adventure. Taking a break from the frenetic pace toward the vision can and should include time to assess your organizational readiness and appetite for a new initiative or strategic journey. Our **Retooling Roadmap** lays out a series of questions to consider what individual and collective skills and resources you have, and in what quantity, to support a new journey.

---

[3] Increasingly, we see articles and research that extoll the benefits of downtime. For example, see: Jackie Coleman and John Coleman, "The Upside of Downtime", *Harvard Business Review*, December 2012; Ferris Jabr, "Why Your Brain Needs More Downtime", October 15, 2013; Steven To, "Benefits of Down Time", *Bright Developers Blog*, May 11, 2017; Joel Falconer, "The Importance of Scheduling Downtime", *LifeHack*, December 28, 2018.

[4] A search of the "link between health and productivity" yields literally millions of hits, including both anecdotal and research-based analysis of the impacts of poor health on individual and organizational performance.

 **ROADMAP**

Assess readiness for the next strategic journey.

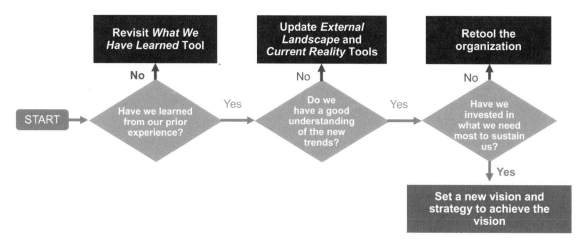

Our **Readiness Assessment Aid** outlines a way to decide whether you can immediately pursue a new destination or should take time to retool. It connects your internal readiness with the external forces that compel you to set a new, aspirational destination. It's a way to focus thinking and highlight areas or opportunities to pursue—or those to avoid. Use the **Organizational Retooling Aid** to decide what investments (in people, equipment, tools, etc.) you will make to replenish and nourish the organization—in the context of what you'll need going forward.

Because you've learned along the way, your new journey will not look exactly like the previous one—even if you successfully reached your destination. Our **Acceleration Tips** suggest ways to make the next journey meaningful for your people and your business.

 AID

Readiness Assessment

Assess our ability to handle the next journey:
Consider our internal readiness vs. external forces.

Step 1. Describe the key trends in your industry

Step 2. Reflect on each trend to decide how urgently you must deal with them, and whether your team is ready to do so

Step 3. Place each trend or opportunity on the matrix (using a symbol) to visualize its position relative to others

Step 4. Consider the implications of this reflection:

- What does it tell you about the opportunities or trends you are most ready to pursue?

- How do you leverage areas of high readiness to support focus areas?

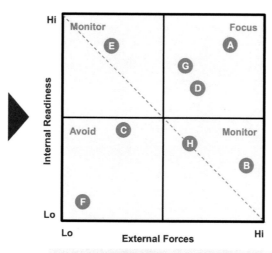

The value of the exercise is in the conversation
– and what you *do* as a result

Internal Readiness

Our ability to handle the next journey

Do we have key positions that are vacant?

Do we have enough capacity to deliver on this and maintain current operations?

Have we sufficiently embedded learnings from the previous journey?

Do we have the energy to pursue this? Do we really want to do this?

Do we have sufficient financial flexibility?

Use binary questions to guide your reflection

External Forces

Opportunities/Threats

Opportunities, threats, or circumstances may compel us to quickly set a new destination:

Are new competitors moving quickly into our space?

Is technology outpacing us?

Do our customers have an urgent need we can fill?

Retooling

Organizational Retooling

Retool the organization in the context of what you used to achieve the vision and what you'll need going forward.

Retooling

Across the organization

	Resources							Action Plan
	Manpower	**Tools**	**Systems**	**Budget**	**Capabilities**	**Processes**	**Etc.**	
Department 1	-	++	-		-			
Department 2	-	--	-					
Department ...	+			++	-	++		
Function 1	-					--		
Function 2	+		+		+			
Function ...	+	+		--				
Etc.								

++	Very Strong
+	Strong
0	Neutral
-	Weak
--	Very Weak

Steps

1. Identify the critical success factors used to reach this destination (See **Gap Analysis Tool** in Section 2)
2. Assess the extent to which each part of the organization has the resources in sufficient quantity and skill to support success
3. Select 2-3 key actions or investments needed to retool

ACCELERATION TIPS

Make the new strategic journey different—yet don't reinvent everything.
- Be clear about what's new and different

Actively solicit external input, including from an advisory board or other experts, to explore new approaches and expand your thinking about the future.

Look for opportunities to leapfrog, based on what you've learned and what competitors are doing (or not).

Consider setting an intermediate or smaller vision rather than requiring another big stretch right away.

Retooling

Conclusion

Reaching the destination is an achievement—whatever your experience has been.

Take a moment to breathe. Then start again. As you set your next destination, revisit the various tools in this book. Your world has changed since you first started. You may have embedded some tools into your ways of working. Or, different tools may be more helpful next time. As you consider your next steps, keep these five principles top of mind:

Without a destination, there is no 'there.'

Strategy is the set of decisions and actions needed to get (there) where you want to go.

Strategy is not linear. You've got to maintain sight of the destination as you set priorities and adapt to changing circumstances.

Metrics connect the dots from priorities to destination. They show progress and support fact-based decisions.

People execute strategy. They deserve explicit attention both individually and collectively.

Place these five concepts at the forefront of your decisions and actions to increase your likelihood for success. Combined, they form the foundation of any strategic journey. They are the most critical building blocks to maintain the balance between strategy and operations—deliberately and constantly.

We'd love to hear more about your experience. Tell us what you learned, what additional discoveries you made, or different gaps or challenges you encountered. Connect with us online at https://Tools4CEOs.com

Acknowledgements

Envisioning the future, developing strategies, and bringing them to life via effective operations and attention to people don't happen in a vacuum. The same is true for this book. We are grateful to the many people who have shaped our experiences and leadership over the years. In one way or another, each of them has been a companion guide, creating the foundation for the practical insights at the heart of our strategic journeys.

Our thanks in particular to former colleagues, mentors, and clients. Each of you left an indelible imprint on the ways in which we have worked, learned, developed others, and led organizations.

Several people provided honest feedback in the very early days of imagining and drafting this toolbox. Thank you, Jennifer Lewis, Beth McDonald, John Hrastar, and Dave Ramos. Mark Levine of Indigo Thinking spent many hours helping us to clarify our story. Your guidance played in our heads as we structured our thinking to be accessible to readers in a book format. New to the publishing process, we are grateful for the early guidance and insight offered by Bob Murray of Style Matters.

To Denise Aranoff, Carol J. Johnson, Gary Magenta, and Lorraine A. Moore: thank you. You generously shared your time, expertise, and perspective to improve both the quality of the text and the way in which we reach our readers. We also appreciate your encouragement and insistence that we persist.

Thank you, Bill Gossman, for reading our manuscript carefully and seeing the value in our tools and approach for CEOs. A successful CEO and entrepreneur many times over, your endorsement means so much to us. Thank you for taking the time to write a compelling foreword which describes how reading this book adds value to an executive's strategic journey.

The book literally would not look like it does without the skill of Linda Popky and her team at Leverage2Market. More than editors and graphic designers, they provided valuable insight to assure this book came to life in the way we hoped.

None of this would have been possible without the persistent, patient attention of our spouses, Fabrice Langreney and Glen Van Zandt. A CEO himself, Fabrice helped us to keep it real. Glen's unfailing willingness to listen and provide blunt feedback kept us on track. Both supported us as we navigated the winding road of creating and publishing a book.

About the Authors

Tara Rethore and **Catherine Langreney** understand the criticality of strategy and the link to operations for a successful business. With the depth and breadth acquired first as senior executives and then, as strategic advisors and coaches, they know that running a business today is complex and ever-changing.

Throughout her career, Tara has led strategy development and execution within large global organizations and as a highly valued consultant. Today, as CEO of Strategy for Real, Tara guides executives, CEOs, and boards in lifting strategy out of the abstract and into action. A recognized expert in strategy, governance, and executive leadership, she brings a global perspective to her clients which include mid-sized organizations in varied industries, nonprofits and associations.
A graduate of Mount Holyoke College, she also earned an MBA from the University of Chicago Booth School.

Tara Rethore

Catherine excels in ensuring that operations are effectively executed against approved strategy. During her 15 years in the construction industry, she led a global division, several country businesses, and a global function for a Fortune 500 company. Today, Catherine has returned to her telecom roots, advising companies operating in Africa. Catherine has served on the boards of public and privately held corporations and several nonprofits. She holds an MS in electrical engineering from ESIEE, in Paris, France, and an MBA from the University of Maryland Smith School.

Catherine and Tara met as executives in a Fortune 500 company, where they were both tasked with driving strategy forward in ways that made sense on the ground. They quickly discovered they had similar ways of thinking, collaborating, and addressing significant, complex business challenges. Both working parents, they also created a lasting bond while navigating the delicate balance of executive leadership and family.

Catherine Langreney

Made in the USA
Las Vegas, NV
20 November 2021